Towards a New Alchemy

The Millennium Science

By Dr. Nick Begich

Earthpulse Press
P. O. Box 201393
Anchorage, Alaska   99520

Printed in the
United States of America

Flanagan Technologies
1109 S. Plaza Way, Suite 399
Flagstaff, AZ 86001
Tel: 602 392 2052

Library of Congress Catalog Number: 96-96347

ISBN 0-9648812-2-5

Cover Art image provided by NASA, Washington, D.C. Diagrams in the text provided by Dr. Patrick Flanagan from his book, _Pyramid Power._

**First Edition
First Printing**

Printed in the United States of America

Anchorage, Alaska

Dedication

This book is dedicated to my wife and children. My family's commitment is the foundation upon which much of my living experience has been built. Also, special thanks to my editors, David Cheezem, James Roderick and Thomas Begich.

This book is also dedicated to Drs. Patrick and Gael Crystal Flanagan, M.D. (M.A.). Half of all royalties from this book are being committed to advancing their work. This book represents the collaborative efforts of our two families.

The purpose of this book is to build upon the ideas first expressed by Dr. Patrick Flanagan in 1973:

If man is to survive in peace with his fellows, he must develop further understanding of life itself and the energies surrounding life. Then he may have a better understanding of his place in the Universe.

About The Author

Dr. Nick Begich is the eldest son of the late United States Congressman from Alaska, Nick Begich Sr., and political activist Pegge Begich. He is well known in Alaska for his political activities. He is a past-president of the Alaska Federation of Teachers and the Anchorage Council of Education. He has been pursuing independent research in the sciences and politics for most of his adult life. Dr. Begich received his doctorate in traditional medicine from The Open International University for Complementary Medicines in November, 1994. He coauthored the book *Angels Don't Play This HAARP; Advances in Tesla Technology* as well as a number of articles on the HAARP project.

Dr. Begich has published articles in the sciences, politics and education and is a well known lecturer. He has been featured as a guest on thousands of radio broadcasts over the last two years in reporting on his research activities. He has also appeared on *Sightings*, BBC-TV in Great Britain and the CBC-TV in Canada.

TABLE OF CONTENTS

CHAPTERS

APPENDIX

Foreword

by Dr. Gael Crystal Flanagan

The very essence of scientific discovery is to show how phenomena in the natural world are inter-dependent and interrelated. This holistic world view points to a universe that is intrinsically dynamic. This web of inter-relationships is a dynamic network of events which includes the human observer and his or her consciousness in a very unique and essential way.

One of the most unique of these human observers of consciousness is my husband: Dr. Patrick Flanagan. When I first heard of Patrick Flanagan it was in relationship to his work with *Pyramid Power*. I was 24 at the time and exploring sacred geometry in depth with a student of Buckminster Fuller, making multi-dimensional geometric models. Patrick's work at that time fit perfectly with what I was doing.

The next time I heard of Patrick's work was in relation to his theory on the structure of water. At that time I was vice president of a company which primarily focused on products to improve the quality of drinking water. Synchronisity strikes again!

Years passed and I found myself co-director of one of the very first holistic health centers in the country. People would come in quite frequently and tell me that so many of our courses resembled in theory what Patrick Flanagan talked about in his lectures on holistic health. There seemed to be a pattern developing in the way our theoretical paths kept crossing.

When we finally met in "real time" it was a case of instant recognition and in less than five months we were married in the King's Chamber of the Great Pyramid of Giza. Life has been a whirlwind of excitement and discovery from the very beginning of our journey together and continues that way to this day.

Patrick is a catalytic blend of energy, intellect and heart. He focuses with laser like intensity when he gives birth to every one of his inventions. This joy of discovery began at a very young age. He was frequently referred to as a child prodigy. Even at a young age his mode of thinking was extremely penetrating, impassioned and spirited. Not many children happen to invent a "guided missile detector" as a science project or the many other inventions he made in the beginning of his work.

Patrick has the special ability to move well beyond everyday perceptions to see the world freshly and rediscover the wonder. People have often referred to Patrick and I as the "Pierre and Marie Curie of the nineties" because as they did, we live, breathe and love our work, giving it to the world as a most treasured gift to use and enjoy.

We see ourselves as a part of a scientific continuum, stretched out in both directions, back to the past and toward an infinite future.

Preface

Reader, brace yourself.

You are about to ride an intellectual and spiritual tornado that will leap across time and space, exploring the contours of science – sometimes touching down lightly, sometimes digging deeply into the discoveries of two amazing scientists/inventors. You will visit the home of a precocious young boy-genius growing up in the quiet, insular Bellaire, Texas of the 1950's, inventing the Neurophone®; you will tour the heady, pioneer laboratories of Listening Incorporated in Boston, where the same young man (though somewhat older) helped develop inter-species communication between dolphins and human beings; and finally, you will discover the vibrant, personal laboratories of Drs. Patrick and Gael Crystal Flanagan in Sedona, Arizona where the researchers continue to explore new inventions as well as new explanations of age-old mysteries. In the mean time, you will take furtive glances into the inner workings of the Pentagon and National Security Agency, as well as the equally mysterious, but much more pleasant, Great Pyramid of Giza, Egypt.

Still, while this ride is necessarily jumpy, you will see new connections in each leap, consistent themes that ride the currents of new knowledge, or as I like to call it, *New Alchemy.*

The word "alchemy" conjures up images of a medieval scientist hidden in a dark room transmuting worthless metal into gold. This may characterize much of the work of the alchemists of old, but it does not tell the whole story. Alchemy is about transformation, change, spiritual energy, but it is also about science, about looking closely at empirical evidence and finding concrete, testable explanations for the mysteries we find. It is about change in thinking, about the use of energy through the medium of the mind – the mind being the intersection of all that is "outside," and all that is "inside" the physical self.

This book is about a new alchemy, about a millennium science. More specifically, it is about two "role models" for those of us interested in opening up these new possibilities: Dr. Patrick Flanagan and Dr. Gael Crystal Flanagan. There will be much more to say about this pair, but it might help to wet the ground with their basic "resumes."

Patrick Flanagan, Ph.D., M.D.(MA) is well known in the scientific community, having been recognized as a child prodigy in physics, electronics and biochemistry. At 14 he invented the Neurophone® and, at 18 was named one of the most promising young scientists in America by _Life_ magazine. He was part of the Gemini Space Program at NASA when he was 19, and at 23, he worked for the U.S. Navy as a computer designer translating human speech into dolphin language for the Man-Dolphin Communications Program. Flanagan is perhaps most famous for his book _Pyramid Power_, about his consuming interest in energy and the bioenergy systems of the human body.

Dr. Gael Crystal Flanagan, M.D.(MA) is an internationally known health researcher, author, inventor, herbalist, and longevity researcher. She has been active in the health field for more than 20 years, co-directing one of the country's first holistic health centers. She is also coauthor of the book, _Elixir of the Ageless_.

Both Patrick and Gael have been exploring the properties of Hunza water, thought to have the most efficient system for delivering nutrients to the cells. Their first Microcluster® product, Crystal Energy®, duplicates the special mineral structures found in Hunza water.

This book represents a compilation of Patrick's ideas and inventions. Each chapter deals with a separate technology and its applications. The vast majority of the material, of course, was compiled through interviews, discussions, written work and other materials they have made available.

The "source material," which is really an outgrowth of our close friendship, has given me much more than the tour of gadgets or even a history of scientific thought; this relationship with the Flanagans has given me a sense that every one of us has a role to play as a catalyst for change. They have renewed my conviction that emerging technologies *can* contribute positively to shifts in human development and balance – *when these technologies are designed to empower rather than enslave human beings.*

Of course, this book is also about some of these "gadgets" or inventions – and I hope to stimulate the commercial pursuit of these ideas, but even if, after reading this book, you find you are not interested in *any* of the Flanagan's inventions, this book will be a success – if you find inspiration from the open-minded pursuit of change that the Flanagan story exemplifies.

Drs. Patrick and Gael Crystal Flanagan.

Chapter 1

The Change

How did it happen that I ended up writing this book? How was it that the circumstances of my life would lead to this work being undertaken? The shift, to a great degree, was stimulated by the transforming affects on myself of friendship and mutual respect.

My life was centered in work which seemed important when I first undertook it ten years earlier. Public service was the focus of much of my family experience and seemed a right course to follow. In the days leading up to my change of focus, it seemed that the world was going to hell in the proverbial hand basket. The politics and union work I was involved in had led to a highway littered with emotional waste. So much energy – so little meaningful change, it seemed everything always found the lowest common denominators of self-interest, cash and power. Where were the altruistic leaders and the vibrant movers in the swill of life? The big picture issues seemed lost in the small things. I was burned-out on the illusion of modern American democracy which, to me, had shifted to special interest domination and alienation of the average person. Public service was lost on most people as self-interest clouded too much of the hidden agendas which where never expressed, just disappointingly discovered.

For me, it was time for a change – a move into a new direction. An accumulation of hundreds of pounds of paper had built up over the years and the clutter needed to be purged. I began to put my file piles into boxes to be shoved into the dark crawl space under my house. It seemed a fitting funeral for musty ideas and spent energy.

Rifling through the documents to be stored I found my science files which had lain idle for almost twelve years. Periodically, I had added to them as I came across something interesting. But, for the most part, they were undisturbed. The science files grew over the years, by default rather than by design, until they occupied a number of boxes. As the emphasis of my occupational work shifted, from union organizing and politics to the sciences, the material I had gathered for two decades would gain increasing significance.

As I thought about the documents and articles, subconsciously sorting them into piles, I felt a sadness, having spent so much time away from the sciences. Years ago, I was beginning work helping friends bring their ideas into the mainstream. At the time, personal and business reversals brought it all to a standstill. Going through the materials I remembered my friend Dr. Reijo Makela, a brilliant scientist. I thought about the ideas he had shared with me twelve years before. In the pile I found a book by the inventor Patrick Flanagan and a few articles about him. I had always felt that these two people were destined to meet. Patrick and Reijo each seemed to possess knowledge which would benefit the others work and, as a consequence, improve the state of the world.

Continuing to sift through the material I couldn't get these guys off of my mind. I kept going back to their writings and the articles. One day, while going through these files I decided, whatever time it took, whatever resources were needed, I was going to relocate Reijo Makela and, somehow, find and meet the mysterious Patrick Flanagan. I spoke with my wife, Shelah, about refocusing my energy into the sciences and told her the story of my old friend Reijo. "Make the change, do what you love and it will work out well", she encouraged. The motion began and the change was set.

It took six months to find Reijo again. As I searched, I began composing a letter to him and compiling materials. As the search for Reijo stretched onward I began to assemble new research material. All of my spare time was committed to reading, research and trying to find my old friend. When I found Reijo again the twelve intervening years had not left him idle. He had moved from basic research into applied technologies, taking his ideas forward in Australia, Europe and Asia. He had developed a new system of acupuncture and had treated over 12,000 people in ten years.

We exchanged our first few letters, which I started to refer to as "Nickpacs" because of their large size. In the exchange I again stumbled onto the Flanagan material and forwarded copies to Reijo. In my own ongoing research, I kept finding references to Patrick Flanagan's work. Then it happened...I was reading a book *Secrets of the Soil*, by Peter Tompkins and Christopher Bird, and in the text there was a chapter about Patrick Flanagan. In the middle of the chapter was a reference to the Open International University for Complimentary Medicines in Sri Lanka which was the same university that Reijo had received one of his doctorate degrees from. This was too coincidental. Here they were, two of the people who's writing and work had influenced me so much passing through the same point. For me it was a confirmation that some effort in locating Dr. Flanagan should begin. It was time for me to find him, introduce Reijo and make myself available to help in their work and in the directions which might be the outgrowth of the effort.

The search for Patrick Flanagan was much easier. I found his name in a database attached to a book and a publisher. It was a common name, in the big picture, so I wondered if it really was the right Patrick Flanagan. I quickly prepared a letter probing for the answer, "Are you the Patrick Flanagan who...." The letter was sent to the publisher's address hoping it was the same Flanagan. What I received back was a form letter from Vortex Industries but it confirmed that I had reached the right person. I needed to pierce the wall of the front desk and get his attention if there was ever to be a meeting. It was important and this was the time. The guts of one of Reijo's most provocative papers was copied and sent. The material was related to some of Dr. Flanagan's areas of scientific interest and, with a short cover letter, it was popped into the mail. Four days later, the phone rang and on the other end was – Dr. Patrick Flanagan.

The phone meeting with Patrick and his research partner and wife Gael was one of the magical transforming moments in my life. Our families spoke together that night for several hours. It was as if we had been friends for a thousand years. We exchanged ideas and in the dialogue we all knew our work would somehow forever be entwined. In the months which followed piles of files were copied and exchanged. Ideas were explored and the phone calls never stopped. I think that in some small ways I help him in his work, and in a profound way, Patrick and Gael changed our lives forever.

It was invigorating and exciting to be stretching into those directions left behind so many years before. The sciences offered so much potential. It was challenging and proved a premise which I continue to maintain – creativity, once recognized, can be turned into any direction or, as my young son Forest would say, it was like switching the channel on a television. Moving from the world of politics and union organizing to the sciences was a radical shift which only my close friends and family could understand.

The work began and would prove to present an endless set of changes and opportunities for personal growth. My parents always emphasized that people were here to serve one another in whatever ways we could. We were put here to help each other reach our full potentials as human beings. I found myself searching for a focus which would actualize my potential and contribute to the work of others in changing the world in some way for the better. My search ended in the sciences and is centered in the friends I found. This book is the outgrowth of those friendships.

Chapter 2

Boy Genius Unquenchable Curiosity

Gillis Patrick Flanagan was born October 11, 1944 in Oklahoma City, Oklahoma to Gillis Chas and Betty Flanagan. From an early age he demonstrated an incredible intellect. He was able to disassemble and reassemble mechanical devices before he was five years old. His curiosity was unquenchable and his determination to satisfy it unstoppable. His parents were supportive of his work even at a young age, believing that his gifts should be developed.

When he was two years old his father gave him a very fine precision Navy compass. His father walked away for a few moments to talk with his mother and when he returned Patrick had completely disassembled the compass. He had removed the tiny screws and separated each part using his hands as his only tools. His parents were mystified by his ability to disassemble the instrument. From that time forward nothing was safe from the curious child. He took everything apart to figure out how it worked. It set the future pattern of his life.

By the age of six he had begun to show an interest in chemistry. His father helped him set up a laboratory in his basement and provided him with chemicals, equipment and books. Within a few years he was studying college-level texts and had acquired a strong working knowledge of chemistry. Through his pursuit of chemistry and learning the periodic table of elements Flanagan became fascinated by the idea that virtually everything in the universe was made out of basic elements. The thought that through molecular manipulation you could create so much variety was astounding to him.

When he was eight years old he developed his own version of the "Russian Sleep Machine". The machine was an electronic device that cause brain waves to slow down. This device put a person into deep sleep, thereby reducing the number of hours needed for a full night's rest. For Patrick this was a great accomplishment, because it left more waking time to pursue his studies. The machine reduced his sleeping hours to four per night.

This is not to say that his experiments always went well. While in elementary school, he was working in his lab on a rocket when the rocket accidentally ignited and lodged itself three inches into a concrete wall. After that event, there was a bit of a family discussion, and he was cautioned to be more careful with his experiments. He was never discouraged from pursuing his interests, however.

As his interests in chemistry grew, he also began to shift his interests into physics and electronics. This interest in chemistry has continued to expand throughout his life. By the time he had reached 14, one of the top chemists for the company his father worked for, Shell Oil Laboratories in Houston, Texas told him that he had the same level of expertise as a graduate in advanced chemistry. He has continued to expand his knowledge of chemistry throughout his life.

His mother encouraged him to develop a well rounded number of interests. As a result, he pursued athletics and showed a particular talent for gymnastics. In gymnastics he won a number of honors and awards throughout high school. Flanagan was not only an intellectual genius and a superb athlete, he was popular as well. In fact, he was elected class president in junior high school.

Patrick entered the Gulf AAU Gymnastics Meet in Houston, Texas in 1963. He first competed as a "Novice Gymnast" in his first competition. The following day he advanced to "Senior All Around Gymnastics Champion" for all of the southern United States. He won over 30 gold medals in his first year of competition.

Patrick has an ability known as "hysterical" or "berserker strength." This means that he can consciously bypass the body's normal protective mechanisms which limit the amount of nerve power which can be transmitted through muscles causing contraction. It is well known that under extraordinary circumstances some people can perform super-human feats of strength.

The reason Flanagan was able to win all of those gymnastic championships was because he was able to break through the pain barrier and perform with incredible strength and control.

When he appeared on the Gary Moore Show on NBC in 1963 he demonstrated his mental/physical power. He laid down on the floor on his stomach, placing his palms flat on the floor by his hips with his elbows in a straight line. He then pressed down on the floor with his hands lifting his body parallel to the floor without bending his arms. He then continued to press his body up into a full handstand.

E. L. Victory, an MIT trained mathematician and physiologist examined Patrick. He determined that Flanagan could produce over 8,000 pounds of force in some muscle groups while switching the force sequentially through twelve different muscle groups in the performance of this feat.

Patrick believes that any person can be taught to "turn on" the hysterical strength survival switch at will.

Flanagan developed an interest in radios and aviation at an early age. At age 11 he received his ham radio license and started a ham club in junior high where he taught fifteen others about radios and many of these individuals went on to become ham operators. As an aviator, he soloed at 16 and shortly after his seventeenth birthday received his private pilot's license.

On December 29, 1962 Flanagan received a Golden Plate Award from the Academy of Achievement in San Diego, California for his invention of the Neurophone®. He was recognized along with several other world-wide achievers for this annual event. It was an honor, and it provided Flanagan an opportunity to meet individuals who would continue to influence his life and who would become life-long friends.[1, 2]

Flanagan was also recognized in the 1962-63 edition of _Leaders in American Science_ which was published by Who's Who in American Education where they made the following special note: "One very interesting feature of Volume V is the inclusion of the biographical sketch and picture of Gillis Patrick Flanagan of Bellaire, Texas. Mr. Flanagan is only eighteen years old and will graduate from high school next June. At this young age he was nationally acclaimed as inventor and scientific genius. We are going to follow his career with great interest." In the text which described Flanagan he was recognized for his bioelectric research and for his work in radio detection of nuclear blasts.

Brain Power

Flanagan has a photographic memory. He can bring back into his memory the visual images of complete pages of material he has read. This ability has allowed him throughout his life to consume vast amounts of information. His personal library contains over 40,000 volumes and represents but a fraction of his studies.

---

[1] Annual Banquet of the Golden Plate of the Academy of Achievement, Program Guide December 29, 1962.

[2] "Achievement Honorees Feted Before Big Salute", Evening Tribune, San Diego, California, December 28, 1962.

While still in high school his reading speed was clocked at 14,500 words per minute with 95% comprehension. Reading at this speed requires a special kind of mental focus which inevitably creates stress and results in physical exhaustion. In the normal course of his work he slows his reading to about 2,000 words a minute while still processing the material in a manner which allows visual recall.

Flanagan also has the ability to use his mind like a blackboard. He has developed this skill over time and it allows him special abilities in contemplating his inventions. He is able to design and redesign his devices in three dimensional color in his mind. He can then use his mental designs to build the devices in his laboratory that day or even years later. Few people have the ability to store and retrieve this kind of material.

Another talent that Patrick has is one of placing himself into the shoes of other inventors. When working on projects which expand or build on the ideas of others he often finds himself lost in an inner world of imagery where he sees through the eyes of the inventor. "It is as if I were there doing the original experiments and seeing their results and future directions of the work," he says. This ability has served him throughout his work in that it allows him the opportunity to see the work as it may have developed years ago and then carry the work of others substantially further, based on his own intuitive insights into the directions of the work. He has been able to use this talent to substantially improve the work of others and to go well beyond the life work of other inventors.

The Dream And the Direction

When Patrick was eight years old he had an unusual dream. It was one of those really rare dreams that some of us might get once or twice in a lifetime. It is when everything is intense and alive and of a nature which defies easy explanation. It is a dream and a concrete reality at the same time. It is a flash of energy which remains inside of the mind forever after the dream has ended. It was such a dream which changed Flanagan's interests from chemistry to electronics.

In his 1952 dream he saw that the world was about to go through a significant technological transformation. He saw this coming change as being significantly more dramatic than the industrial revolution. What he saw was the coming of an age where the power of the mind would greatly expand and electronics and computers would dominate the age. In his dream he saw himself making great contributions to this coming revolution in technology.

The dream was startling and surprising to Patrick. The electronics and computer industries were just barely beginning to take the form which they now have. The few computers which existed at the time were huge cumbersome machines which took up thousands of square feet and yielded little in comparison to the computers of today. Modern desk top units such as the one being used to compose this book would have outperformed everything that was operating at the time.

From the day of the dream onward his interests shifted to physics and electronics. He read whatever he could find on the subjects, devouring dozens upon dozens of volumes. It was strange in a way as he read because it was as if much of the material he found was a refresher rather than new knowledge. It was as if he already knew much of the material. It made the reading and study easy and exciting. As he read he continued to experiment, designing and building his first electronic circuits at age eight and completely building his own radio transmitter/receiver from a pile of parts at age ten.

Guided Missile Detector

At age 11, he was designing and building gadgets of various kinds. At 12 he completed work on a guided missile detector.3   The device which he designed was portable and could detect missile firings and atomic bomb blasts up to 8,000 miles away within an instant of the lift-off or detonation. He built the detector using spare parts from a Ham radio and $5.00 in new components. An article in the _Houston Post_ described the device and its construction.4 Flanagan considered the system design pretty simple and not such a big deal, however, military engineers considered it superior to their significantly larger and more expensive designs. The Flanagan design was such that it could be modified even for satellite use.

He knew that when a large rocket took off it created an unusual effect. The exhaust would produce such high temperatures that it would ionize the escaping gases which would in turn send out very low frequency energy waves which could travel completely around the earth. The trail of exhaust would create an antenna of ionized gases radiating energy. Using a receiver, he was able to isolate the signal, detecting the time and direction of the rocket launches. The same kind of low frequency energy pulse was also created by atomic blasts and his device could also detect these signals. He could detect atomic blasts as far away as Nevada, the Soviet Union or the South Pacific.

Over the next three years he recorded all of the major missile firings and atomic test blasts conducted world-wide. He entered the Houston city-wide Science Fair with his device and won the top award for both electronics and for the Science Fair overall. Two weeks later an article appeared in the _Houston Post_ regarding the invention. Immediately, other news papers and magazines from around the world picked up the story and published their own accounts of this remarkable young inventor. Several days later, Patrick was sitting in one of his eighth grade classes when the principal announced over the school public address system; "Attention! Will

3 "Boy's Missile Detector Wins science Fair", Electronics, October 16, 1959.
4 "8th Grader Scores; Boy's Missile Finder Attracts Corporation", by Ron Moskowitz, Houston Post. April, 1962.

Patrick Flanagan come to my office immediately. The Pentagon is on the telephone." Flanagan was stunned. His classmates were shocked. He had occasionally raised a few eyebrows with his experiments...but the Pentagon was calling?

It was true, the general on the telephone said, "Son, we want to know how you know all about these atomic tests and missile firings." He explained how his instruments worked and how he had developed the designs. Within days be was visited by officers from the Air Research and Development Command who continued the probes for detailed information on the technology he had developed. Then as quickly as the visits began, they ended. The project was classified as Top Secret and they would not discuss it with him further. It was just a few months later that the United States government announced the deployment of a new device which would detect all missile firings and atomic tests. The new device was to be located on satellites.

Exciting? Sure it was. But by the time of the dramatic phone call, the detection device was already three years old. Patrick had moved on to a new, perhaps more significant invention: The Neurophone®.

Chapter 3

Electronic Telepathy The Neurophone®

The Neurophone® was invented the year I was born. It went through numerous advances before I met Patrick and had an opportunity to try the invention. The device changed from a crude sound system to one which delivered clear and consistent sound quality.

A year ago my wife, Shelah and I took a trip to Sedona, Arizona to visit the Flanagans and try the Neurophone® and the Neurophone® Pink Noise Generator.

Patrick had already explained how the invention worked, treating the skin as an eardrum – actually using the nervous system to transfer the sound to the brain. We were eager to try it, and we connected with the Flanagans as soon as we were settled into our hotel.

Soon the Flanagans greeted us in person with a classical music CD and early prototypes of the Neurophone® and the Neurophone® Pink Noise Generator. Once the device was hooked up Patrick handed me the two electrodes and said, "place them anywhere on your skin." I placed the electrodes between my thumbs and forefingers and instantly I could hear the music as if it were playing in the center of my head. At the same time, I could hear the sounds like a faint scratchy noise coming from the place the electrodes were located on my body. This was a secondary effect which occurred as the information was being transferred into my skin. At the location of the electrode contact with my fingers the electromagnetic currents had made my skin act like a little speaker directly under the electrode. The sound quality I heard was scratchy but clear in my head. Flanagan said that as the new pathways are being formed for the transfer of sound information the signal would get clearer. He said that for most people an hour use per day for a week would smooth out the signal and improve the sound quality.

I moved the electrodes around to different parts of my body and the signal was always the same – I could hear the music in the center of my head. It was amazing and defied any sense of what was supposed to happen with sound and hearing. I realized that this invention truly was incredible. I played with the device throughout the evening as we talked about its potential.

The Newtech Tool

The Neurophone® is an electronic device which transmits sound through the skin to the brain, by-passing the normal hearing channels. The device converts sound waves into digitized electronic signals which have a wave form and timing configuration, which can be deciphered and understood by the human brain. The internal hearing, or mental sound printing, is delivered to the brain intact just as it was transmitted. The electronic signal is fully perceptible as if the sound were heard through the ears. The sound is sound except it is as if it were emanating from inside a person's head. The artificially induced sound is electronically coded and transferred to the brain where the signal is understood and decoded. Simply put, the device can take any sound including speech and music and convert it to a signal which the human body can receive and transfer through the skin.

The human body works in conjunction with the man-made apparatus recreating the original sound whether it was generated from a microphone, tape recorder, CD player, or other sound signaling device. Any sound input device can be used. The Neurophone®

alters the sound signal into the equivalent of "brain computer code" which, when sent and reconstructed by the brain, is understood as specific sounds. It is not a series of beeps, clicks or vibrations; it is the actual words and sounds reconstructed in the brain just as if they were heard through the ears.

This was the second most significant invention of Patrick Flanagan's after his missile and atomic blast detector. The story which follows was put together from a number of published reports on the device and from many hours of conversations with Patrick Flanagan.

The Idea Is Born

The Neurophone® was invented in 1958 when Flanagan was 14 years old and living in Bellaire, a suburb of Houston, Texas. The idea for the invention was stimulated when he read a science fiction book written in 1911 by Hugo Gernsback, the founder of Gernsback Publications. In the book, Ralph 124C41+, the hero had an electronic telepathy machine which could program information directly into the brain. The idea of electronic telepathy intrigued Flanagan and his work on the first Neurophone® began.

When working models of the Neurophone® were demonstrated and announced, the news media immediately picked up the story. At the time of its announcement, it created an uproar in the media and reached the pages of over 300 newspapers in one day. Life magazine did a feature article on Flanagan and his Neurophone® in 1962 when he was 18 years old.[5] The article described Flanagan and his invention. After the article appeared he was offered eight million dollars for the invention by corporate executives who wanted to develop the idea into applied technologies. Flanagan turned this offer down.

---

[5] <u>Life</u> magazine, "Whiz Kid, Hands Down", William Moeser, September 14, 1962, pages 69 & 72.

The first Neurophone®.

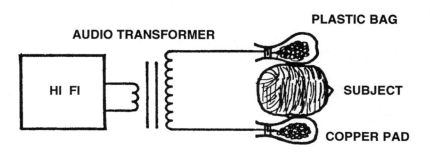

Early experimental Neurophone

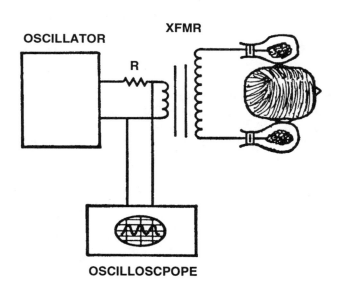

Measuring Resonance

The U.S. Patent Office was the first battle for Patrick Flanagan in getting his Neurophone® into production. With the help of a friend who was a patent attorney for Shell Oil Company, Flanagan drew his own diagrams, wrote his own patent application and submitted it. While the patent application was being reviewed the invention was gaining publicity. It was at this point that the patent examiners started giving the young inventor problems. The examiners claimed that the device could never work and refused to issue the patent. They said that the invention was not really what Flanagan had characterized it to be. They said that the phenomena he was seeing was the result of old unpatented knowledge of bone resonant transfer. The refusal of the patent led to a battle of paper flying through the mail. In the end it appeared all for naught as the application was denied and the file permanently closed.

In anger and out of desperation Flanagan and his lawyer flew to Washington D.C. with a working model of the device. Although the file had been closed the examiner agreed to listen to the duo and consider what they had to present. The examiner also had a surprise in store for Flanagan to test his invention. The examiner had arranged for a deaf employee to be available for the meeting. The gentleman was totally nerve deaf in one ear and almost totally deaf in the other. Flanagan hooked the fellow up to the Neurophone® and played the voice of Maria Callas singing an opera. As the invention was activated, and the music started playing, the man sat quietly at first and then tears began streaming down his face. The joy broke through as if he had been reborn, he could hear the clear precision of the operatic voice. The man loved opera but had not had the pleasure of the sound except in the fading memories of his mind. Then here, in a dingy government office, the crisp clear penetrating voice again played vividly in his mind in the new vibration of neurophonic sound. As a result of this experience and in a most unusual series of events, the file was reopened and the patent granted. Up until this time the Patent Office had never reopened a file after it had been officially closed. The patent application was promptly processed and the patent issued for the first Neurophone®.

The Amazing Patent

The following paragraphs are Flanagan's description of the Neurophone®.These descriptions were taken from the text of the patents and serve to illustrate the claims which the United States Patent Office accepted, in the end, as valid for the technology he discovered:

"This invention relates to electromagnetic excitation of the nervous system of a mammal and pertains more particularly to a method and apparatus for exciting the nervous system of a person with electromagnetic waves that are capable of causing that person to become conscious of information conveyed by the electromagnetic waves."[6]

"It is an object of the present invention to provide a means of initiating controllable responses of the neuro senses without applying pressure waves or stress waves to the ears or bones. Another object of this invention is to provide a means of causing a person to receive an aural perception of the sound corresponding to the audio modulation of radio frequency electromagnetic waves that are coupled with the nervous system of the person."[7]

"In the method of the present invention, a response is initiated in the nervous system of a mammal by disposing at least a portion of that nervous system within a field of electromagnetic waves of a radio frequency above the aural range. In a preferred embodiment of this invention, the field to which the nervous system is exposed is a field containing modulated electromagnetic waves of a particular radio frequency to which the individual nervous system is selectively responsive. In a particularly preferred embodiment of this

6 United States Patent Number 3,393,279 issued to Gillis Patrick Flanagan July 16, 1968.
7 Ibid.

invention, at least a portion of the nervous system of a person is exposed to audio modulated electromagnetic waves having a radio frequency such that the person experiences the sensation of hearing, substantially free of distortion, the information which is conveyed by the audio modulation."[8]

"The present invention may be used as a hearing aid, as an aid to teaching speech to a person who is born deaf, as a means of communicating with persons in locations in which the noise level is high, as a device by which a person can listen to an audio signal that cannot be heard by others, etc."[9]

The apparatus "has been used to communicate speech and music to numerous persons including registered physicians. In these uses the electrodes, in the form of circular discs covered by plastic insulation, were placed against the sides of the heads of the persons. When electromagnetic waves were adjusted to a frequency to which persons having normal hearing were selectively responsive, none of these persons perceived any sensations of hearing or experienced any discomfort when no audio modulation was applied to the waves. When the waves were audio modulated with speech or music signal, none of these persons experienced any discomfort, but they each had the sensation of listening to the transmitted information and 'hearing' it at least as clearly as they would hear such information from an audible transmitter. When the same apparatus was similarly employed on a person whose hearing had been damaged to an extent requiring a hearing aid to hear normal conversation, that person 'heard' the audio signal (with hearing aid disconnected) and 'heard' music with a better fidelity than that obtainable with his hearing aid."[10]

"I claim: 1. A method of transmitting audio information to the brain of a subject through the nervous

8 United States Patent Number 3,393,279 issued to Gillis Patrick Flanagan July 16, 1968.
9 Ibid.
10 Ibid.

system of the subject which method comprises, in combination, the steps of generating a radio frequency signal having a frequency in excess of the highest frequency of the audio information to be transmitted, and applying said modulated radio frequency signal to a pair of insulated electrodes and placing both of said insulated electrodes in physical contact with the skin of said subject, the strength of said radio frequency electromagnetic field being high enough at the skin surface to cause the sensation of hearing the audio information modulated thereon in the brain of said subject and low enough so that said subject experiences no physical discomfort."

"2. The method of claim 1 wherein said modulated electromagnetic field is coupled with a portion of the nervous system contained in the person's spinal column."

"3. Apparatus for transmitting audio information to the brain of a subject through the nervous system of the subject comprising, in combination, means for generating a radio frequency signal having a frequency greater than the maximum frequency for said audio information, means for modulating said radio frequency signal with the audio information to be transmitted, electrode means adapted to generate a localized radio frequency electromagnetic field thereabout when excited by a radio frequency signal, and means coupling said modulated radio frequency signal to said electrode means, said electrode means having a surface adapted to be capacitively coupled to a localized area at the surface of the skin of said subject when placed in physical contact therewith whereby said electrode means may generate a localized radio frequency electromagnetic field modulated by said audio information at the surface of the skin of said subject, and means on said surface of said electrode means for insulating said electrode means from the skin of said subject." [11]

---

11 United States Patent Number 3,393,279 issued to Gillis Patrick Flanagan July 16, 1968.

The second patent went further in explaining the invention, how it worked, and what might be possible with the technology. In the patent Flanagan said:

"This invention relates generally to electronic processing of speech, and more particularly relates to a method and system for simplifying the speech waveform to facilitate transmission of the speech through various media without materially degrading intelligibility." 12

The average person does not consider speech as a "waveform". In fact we really don't think much about speech at all in terms of what it is specifically. In the case of this invention it simplified the waveform in such a way as to allow for clear transmission over significant distances through air, water, or land. The value of this transmission technology was significant not only for communications systems that we all are aware of such as public address systems, radio or other sound transmitting systems; this new system of transmitting or coding the sound had a significant impact on the possibilities presented by the Neurophone®. This second patent was the key to effective Neurophonic technology.

"In the process of producing human speech, the voice box creates a series of sound pulses which reverberate within and are shaped by the upper throat and mouth cavity. The frequency of the pulses produced by the voice box primarily determine the frequency or pitch of the sound, while the shape of the mouth cavity reverberates and shapes the sound to produce speech information. The resulting speech waveform is very complex and highly redundant. If such a waveform is passed through a band-pass filter having a bandwidth significantly less than 3,000 cycles per second, the speech becomes unintelligible. Thus, even the simplest voice communication channels require a substantial bandwidth. Heretofore it has been commonly believed that the speech information was contained in the amplitude as well as the frequency modulation of the

---

12 United States Patent Number 3,647,970.

speech waveform. When voice sounds are induced in a body of water or the earth, the many reverberations caused by the various velocity discontinuities make speech unintelligible over relatively short transmission lengths. Also, the complete speech waveform has made encoding or scrambling for secure transmissions, either by electromagnetic, electrical, or pressure waves, so impractical as to be very seldom used."[13]

The patent, in simple terms, was for a system which would change speech into a waveform which could more completely and readily be transmitted over long or short distances and then be received and reconfigured into the original sound.

In a confidential disclosure of the invention which accompanied the patent application the invention was described as a "square wave speech digitizer" which was described as follows:

"This invention is a digitizing technique which, while retaining full speech intelligibility, removes from the spoken message all amplitude variations, resulting in an on/off code."

"This code is so remarkable, that although when viewed on an oscilloscope, it appears to be a series of square waves, it remains fully intelligible without further processing...i.e., it may be transmitted to any number of mechanical transducing systems normally used for speech, and it retains its full intelligibility."

"This system then simplifies speech itself, the simplified speech can perform very simply many many tasks normally requiring very complex equipment...a few examples are: 95% efficient amplifiers, radio transmitter modulators, underwater communication systems, 100% efficient laser modulators, very narrow band radio systems, and speech controlled machinery."

---

13 United States Patent Number 3,647,970.

One of the other and primary capabilities of this invention included the ability to devise highly specialized secured communications systems which would be easy to use and almost impossible to decode. This was, perhaps, one of the primary reasons that the United States military would place the invention under a National Secrecy Order.

Confiscation of Intellectual Property
The National Security Order

On August 29, 1968 – a month after the first patent had been issued – Patrick Flanagan applied for the second Neurophone® patent. He had made some new changes, dramatically improving the consistency of the Neurophone®. This new patent was the link which would create the most incredible combination: A digital, self-adjusting, real time, feedback device. This device was designed to deliver sound, coded for the brain, to a person in a way which was fully discernible to the individual. This new invention provided a necessary ingredient needed to bring the Neurophone® into production.

Patrick expected the new patent to move through the process easily; instead, he faced his greatest obstacle to date: The Defense Intelligence Agency seized the patent information. The official word that the patent application was sealed with a secrecy order was sent to Flanagan on April 25, 1969. This effectively kept the patent from being approved until March 7, 1972. It seemed that after the first patent had been issued that the Defense Intelligence Agency had also become convinced of the effectiveness of the Neurophone® and that they saw secret applications for this new technology. The secrecy order number was 756,124 (in 1968) which indicated that by that time there had already been over three quarter million intellectual confiscations by the federal government.

The national security order forbade Patrick from

talking about the technology, promoting the idea, or working further on the invention. These restrictions are enforced by the United States Justice Department.

The application that the government was seeking was related to controlling human behavior. At the time the government, through the Central Intelligence Agency (CIA), was engaging in illegal activities testing these technologies on Americans and others.14 They were developing methods of mind control using LSD, hypnosis and other means. It was likely that this was the use they sought through this new electronic technology. During this same period there was substantial work being done by United States intelligence agencies on these kinds of technologies.

After the famous Watergate break-in was engineered with the help of the CIA, a special investigation was launched into the activities of the agency. The Commission on CIA Activities Within the United States was formed and chaired by Nelson A Rockefeller. Two of the other committee members were Ronald Reagan and Lane Kirkland, who would later reach prominence as President of the United States and President of the AFL-CIO, the most powerful labor confederation in the world. The CIA was concerned about the techniques which were used by the Soviets and Koreans in "brainwashing" prisoners of war and others. In the text of the Commission's report it was disclosed that besides the use of LSD on unsuspecting Americans they also engaged in other activities. "The drug program was a part of a much larger program to study possible means for controlling human behavior. Other studies explored the effects of radiation, electric-shock, psychology, psychiatry, sociology and harassment substances."15 The US government had captured a brain manipulating electronic device called a Lida machine during the Vietnam War. This Soviet made device would

14 Report to the President by the Commission on CIA Activities Within The United States, U.S. Government Printing Office Stock Number 041-015-00074-8, Issued June 1975.
15Ibid.

electronically put prisoners in a trance state during interrogations. The idea of electronic interrogation was of great interest to the US intelligence community and the Neurophone® was thought to be a major part of this new wave of technology.

In the United States, the government can confiscate intellectual property without fair compensation. This is in conflict with the Constitution in terms of its private property right provisions. The United States Constitution established provisions for fair and just compensation for the confiscation of private property. However, these kinds of confiscations were only able to be executed by the federal government under very limited circumstances. These Constitutional provisions were established as a result of pre-Revolutionary War abuses, by British troops who seized the property of farmers for military purposes without compensating them. Seizures would also occur when troops would require temporary lodging while passing through an area and would fail to compensate property owners for food, housing or other resources they consumed. The owners were treated as servants of the crown in these kind of property abuses and this kind of action by the British government was one of the contributing factors to the Revolutionary War.

In a technological age the problem isn't the property of farms only; it now includes the intellectual property of people who represent the new minds for change. Knowledge is change. The freedom of speech, press and beliefs is foundational and yet, in America, under a National Security Order, property can be taken without fair recourse for the inventor. While it is true that the property of the mind has changed in two hundred years, its right of ownership has not. Where does the federal government draw the line? Why should people be denied the right to pursue their inventiveness without undue restraint by the government?

The founding fathers of the United States determined that even in war situations property should not be taken without fair payment. Since World War II, intellectual property has increasingly fallen into the government confiscation void creating significant hardship on the part of inventors while depriving the world of access to the fruits of their human creativity. The ever increasing and indiscriminate use of "national security" seizures of knowledge goes beyond what was ever envisioned as possible two hundred years ago. The idea that thought itself would be confiscated by our federal government was never anticipated or contemplated, as a possibility in the consciousness of those who established our form of government. In fact, the freedom to say, to believe, to express and to amplify ideas was the most foundational aspect of our system of human interaction as exemplified in American republican democracy. Nonetheless, in 1996 we face ever increasing intrusions on individual inventors by a government with a million lawyers on the payroll, funded with hundreds of billions of dollars and able to tie up individuals in a web of regulation and control, strangling freedom of thought. These same intrusions also accrue to the government tremendous power which is often used to the detriment of humankind rather than its improvement.

Knowledge should not be restricted when it can be applied to the general good of people. National security interests must be balanced. The question which must be asked is: who's interests are served by withholding this kind of knowledge? And who are these non-elected, unappointed, thought-police who are standing guard over the intellects of creative Americans? Intellectual knowledge restriction is a modern outcome of cold war paranoia. The question which is currently crystallizing in the minds of many individuals is; where does the government interference end and the pursuit of life, liberty and happiness begin?

There are too many times when we draw artificial barriers between human interactive events like science and politics, as if they were just "islands of action" unto themselves, when, in reality, all things are interconnected. Restrictions of inventor property rights only affect a handful of people directly because it does not happen often. It is relatively easy for the government to trample on a few disenfranchised inventors who can either work for the government or go through a seemingly unending barrage of hogwash dished out by overly aggressive bureaucrats. The government can perpetuate these injustices because the mass of the American population does not see it as "their" issue. So what if a few independent scientists get tied up and can't get their ideas into production and available to people? What is missed, in these withdrawals into apathy, is the fact that these suppressed ideas may offer all people, or significant numbers of people, other more positive possibilities. Withholding learning technologies, healing systems and other knowledge which can improve human conditions is an act of betrayal against the human spirit and a democratic way of life.

Knowledge is freedom and freedom to create are foundations of democracy. Moreover, the confiscation of property for application in military purposes may run counter to an inventor's religious or philosophical beliefs in terms of warfare and human interaction. Does the government have the right to take property from an inventor and use it for military applications when the inventor's philosophy forbids this kind of use? What right does a government have to take what others have created, and interfere with the inventor's ability to continue to develop his ideas? Apparently, in the United States, national security organizations can achieve this end and this is what happened to the Neurophone® and Patrick Flanagan.

The effect on society is profound. In areas where it is time to advance technologically we are forced, as societies, to wait until the government decides the knowledge is either "suitable" for consumption or has become widespread enough so that the continued denial of the information is no longer worthwhile. In the interim, progress by the originators of the ideas is delayed, lost or put off indefinitely; such was almost the case with the Neurophone®.

Back To the Beginning

When Flanagan was 15 years old he gave a lecture and demonstration of the Neurophone® to the Houston Amateur Radio Club. The day after the demonstration, he was contacted by a reporter from the *Houston Post*. The reporter had a relative who had become nerve deaf from spinal meningitis, and he wanted to try the invention on his relative. The test was arranged. The device worked as expected, causing a cascade of news reports. The story hit the international wire services and the publicity on the device grew substantially over the next two years. At one point, in 1961, staff from *Life* magazine descended on Flanagan's family home for a week, following him through his days while compiling a story on the boy-genius. On September 14, 1962 the story appeared in the magazine.

After the Life Magazine story Patrick was invited to appear on the Gary Moore show, "I've Got a Secret." During the October 1, 1962 filming of the show, the Neurophone® was demonstrated with the help of two other guests, Andy Griffith and Bess Meyerson. As a result of this television appearance Flanagan received over one million letters and telegrams on the device.

After the show Patrick met Andrija Puharich. Dr. Puharich took Flanagan and G. Harry Stine, a scientist working for Huyck Corporation, to lunch to discuss the Neurophone®. Puharich was pursuing a similar patent to Flanagan's and he was trying to extract information from the young Flanagan. Later Flanagan would have to fight Puharich in litigation over the rights to the idea. But the record would be clear: Flanagan had filed for the patent first.

After the Gary Moore appearance, Flanagan was also contacted by the Huyck Corporation, the research company Stine worked for. Flanagan hired on as a consultant during the summers and worked with the firm in conducting further research on his invention. The company was able to verify the effectiveness of the Neurophone®, but because of the problems and delays from the patent office the project was dropped.

While working for the Huyck Corporation, Flanagan was able to meet a number of other research scientists who would have a profound impact on his future directions. He met Dr. Henri Marie Coanda, the father of fluid dynamics and got to know Harry Stine better. Harry Stine was to write a book about the potential use of the Neurophone® as a human to computer interface device. The book was called _The Silicon Gods,_ (Bantam Books). Dr. Coanda was to stimulate future research directions for Patrick.

The next stage of research on the Neurophone® began when Flanagan was twenty-three and was employed as a research scientist at Tufts University. While working at Tufts, he served as Vice President in charge of research for Listening Incorporated, a Boston based company. Listening Incorporated was set up to develop a number of technologies and was under contract to the United States Naval Ordinance Test Station out of China Lake, California. The Navy had contracted Flanagan's company to develop a number of technologies including systems for interpreting man-to-dolphin speech. The senior scientist on the project was his friend and business partner at the time, Dr. Dwight Wayne Batteau, a Professor of Physics and Mechanical Engineering at Harvard and Tufts Universities.

At Tufts, Flanagan continued to develop his ideas. While there he decoded speech intelligence patterns as they are replicated in the brain of humans and dolphins in order to develop the computer programs to analyze and simulate them. During this research Flanagan and the others discovered the way in which the brain locates things in three dimensional space so that even when you couldn't see the location of the sound you could still locate it. Reversing this concept they found a method for projecting sound into locations within three dimensional space. In this way, they could recreate even the direction of sound so that the voice of an orchestra could be perceived in its full width and depth of sound as if standing in front of live instruments. A totally different rhythm - holographic sound projection was discovered.

This sound technology, and the research comprising it, led to increased understanding of the time ratio relationships of the brain-speech recognition systems. This understanding of the projection of sound into three-dimensional space, and the idea surrounding the timing ratios of the brain's speech recognition circuitry allowed for the development of a digitized Neurophone®.

The new digital Neurophone® produced the ultimate sound. A sound inside the head with the precision fidelity of an orchestra. The sound could be both recoded and projected through the energy grid network of the human body. *The device plugs directly into the neuro-network, which forms the human computer, in such a way so as to project information into the total experiential brain.* A machine-to-human download into long-term memory. The shifting of information into long term memory after even just one application was proven to be possible for many users of the device.

This new combination of ideas led to the August 29, 1968 patent application filing for the new and powerful technology which was quickly sealed by the Defense Intelligence Agency for five years. The sealing of this patent was incredibly agonizing. The 24 year old inventor had worked so long to get the first idea patented. He had fought the patent office, patent infringement litigation and now a national security order forbidding him from working on, or even talking about, the invention. The battle for the right to his work went five years until the government reluctantly rescinded the order. By then, a good deal of the enthusiasm for the

Neurophone® was lost to the inventor and he had moved on to other projects.

Still, Patrick did manage to produce about 1,500 Neurophones® which sold for $1,000 each in 1978-79. The device was large and bulky and the price of the device was necessarily high but beyond the capabilities of the average person. Flanagan decided that he would discontinue the manufacture of the device until it could be made more affordable and when he could assure that it would be marketed in the way he had envisioned.

The First Neurophone® is Built

The first Neurophone® was created using the technojunk that a child had collected around the house. A stop at the cabinet under the kitchen sink and to the kitchen pantry yielded the steel wool electrodes for the device, which were inserted into plastic sandwich bags and connected to insulated copper wires. The wires from the steel wool electrodes were connected to a reversed audio transformer which was in turn connected to a record player. The output voltage of the audio transformer was 1,500 volts peak-to-peak. The signal from the electrical energy wave was viewed on an oscilloscope used for looking at wave forms and electrical outputs. The amplifier was driven by either music or voice inputs from the record player or as they used to be called the Hi-Fi. (Today, any sound recording device could be used including a CD player, cassette recorder, etc.)

The electrodes were placed on the temples, next to the eyes, and when the Neurophone® was clicked on you could "hear" the sounds as if they were originating inside your head. The sound quality with this first generation device was weak, distorted and generally of poor quality. The first generation device produced an interesting effect but was of no practical value because of this poor sound quality, which was related to the encoding of the signal. Using the device, and monitoring the outputs, Flanagan discovered that some sound signals were more clear than others.

While looking at the oscilloscope it was discovered that the clearest and loudest sounds could be generated when the amplifier was over-driven and square waves were being produced. At the same time, the transformer would ring or oscillate with a dampened wave form at frequencies of 40-50 kilohertz (kHz). What Patrick found was that under certain conditions the signal could not be perceived at all and other signals came through very clearly. By isolating the clearer signals and analyzing their modulations Flanagan was able to determine the ideal operating parameters of the device.

Flanagan went to the library to research the effect he had observed and see if there had been any historic mention of the phenomena. What he discovered was that a similar effect was first recognized by a scientist, Volta, as far back as 1800. At the time of its discovery, it was called electrophonic hearing and was thought to be merely a phenomenon which was created by action of the muscles surrounding the bones of the inner ear being stimulated to vibrate by an electric current thereby causing the hearing effect.

Flanagan continued his research and observations in order to try and better define the mechanism by which the phenomenon actually occurred. While observing the signal on the oscilloscope, he found that the sound was transmitted to the brain only when the transformer became overloaded, creating a blast of spiked electrical energy which then resonates through the body to the brain. This resonance effect helped explain why the sound signal only passed through partially and not all sounds would transmit clearly. In order to transmit clearly they had to be resonating in harmony with the skin.

The human body actually was forming part of the electrical circuit for the device. The body was not acting like some kind of empty water pitcher waiting for the next fill up; it was serving as a part of the circuit itself.

Flanagan designed a circuit utilizing this knowledge and created a high frequency oscillator for sending the signal through the human neuro-network energy grid. But then he discovered that the particular resonant frequency of an individual person was subject to significant electrical changes and other variables. The electrical properties of the skin were such that general body changes, emotional changes, and virtually any outside stimulant could cause a shift in electrical properties. The shift caused the device to function erratically; it could not be readily controlled to match these shifting energy patterns. The dielectric properties of the skin could change by many magnitudes in a fraction of a second. This became both the challenge and the obstacle for the young scientist in refining his invention.

The device at this point (just as the original patent was being prepared) was essentially a high voltage, low power frequency modulated radio transmitter, with the frequency manually adjusted to match the natural frequencies of the human body. To understand how the device worked, it would be helpful to review what happens when you turn on a "tune" a radio:

> 1) The receiver dial is turned until a resonating match between the broadcast signal resonates with the tuned frequency of the radio, and;
>
> 2) The signal is decoded and sent through the speaker as sound.

With the Neurophone®, the human body acts as a radio receiver. The electrical impulses are "received" by the nerves through the skin, transferred to the brain, and decoded into sound.

The Neurophone® system works by taking the sound from a CD player, tape recorder or microphone and changing it to a signal that is continually modulated to meet the shifting energy of the human body. The shifting, self-correcting modulations cause the device to stay in tune with the individual so that the converted sound information can be continuously downloaded into the brain where it is received in the same way as a radio broadcast. Flanagan described the effect this way: "The sound from the device was fantastic, like sound from another world." The sound quality and range of "hearing" was extended well beyond the normal hearing parameters of the ear and there was no distortion in the signal being received as there was in the first generation of the device.

At this time Flanagan began testing the device on individuals who were totally nerve deaf. These individuals were not able to hear through the normal hearing channel or through bone conduction methods. The results of these trials were incredible. People could hear for the first time!

The Second Generation Neurophone®

The second generation Neurophone® was constructed out of a variable frequency vacuum tube oscillator that was amplitude-modulated. The output signal was then fed into a high frequency transformer which was flat in frequency response in the 20-100 kHz range. The electrodes were placed on the head and the oscillator was tuned for the maximum resonance (Later models had a feedback circuit built in which automatically adjusted the frequency for resonance.) Flanagan found that the dielectric constant of human skin was highly variable and in order to achieve a maximum energy transfer from the electrodes the unit required constant retuning in order to match the dynamic electric response of the body of the listener.

With the second generation Neurophone® a 2,000 volt peak-to-peak amplitude-modulated carrier wave was then connected to the body using a two inch diameter electrode disc which was insulated using mylar films of various thicknesses.

The Neurophone® is a scalar wave generator. In operation, the out-of-phase signals from the electrodes mix in the non-linear complexities of the skin dielectric. The signals from each capacitor electrode are 180 degrees out of phase. Each signal is transmitted into the complex dielectric of the human body where it is mixed and phase cancellation takes place. The net result is a scalar vector.

The second generation Neurophone®, with its high frequency amplitude-modulated improvements, was an incredible advancement over the one developed earlier. It had excellent sound clarity. The listener perceived the sound as if it were emanating from inside his head. This device was tested on over 1,000 people, including some who were nerve deaf. The results were startling. In some instances, for unknown reasons, the listener could not hear with the device until it was used is a series of short sessions. We are not sure why some people need this "training period," but our best guess is that the nervous system needs to "learn" to hear with the device, to build the neuro pathways from the skin to the brain, and to decode the new kind of impulse.

The device also caused some unexpected visual images when it was activated while being placed over the occipital region of the brain. The idea that this device might also be tunable in such a way as to create visual imaging suggests that it may be possible for this purpose in the future. The possibility of finding a mechanism for a visual Neurophone® was not lost on the inventor and is the subject of further research. Visual imaging may be created using other than the optical imaging created by the eyes.

Recent research has shown that when the blind are using braille the actual areas of the brain which are stimulated are those associated with sight rather than those associated with touch. In addition, research conducted in the former Soviet Union showed that a system for visual imaging through the skin was possible. The research was with highly sensitive individuals who were able to learn to distinguish objects, letters and even pictures using their hands as optical image scanners.16 What is now known is that it may be possible to isolate the mind-brain-code for distinguishing visual images in much the same way as the auditory code is used with the Neurophone®.

The applications of the ideas sounding the continued advancement of Neurophone® technology are incredible. The commercial possibilities are enormous. The applications include sound production and recording equipment and Neurophone® sound dimensionalizers. These are the learning, and listening system, which outpace other devices by a hundred years. The first digitized Neurophone®, used for these purposes, was eventually manufactured and marketed as the Mark XI and the Thinkman Model 50 versions.

How the Neurophone® Works

The skin is the largest and most complex part of our physical form. Spread out, our skin would cover about forty square feet and weigh nine pounds making it the largest organ in the body.17   It stands between us and the outer world. It is the first barrier between disease and ourselves and acts as a giant liquid crystal brain. Every square inch of the skin contains 1300 pain receptors, nearly 20,000 touch receptors, almost 200 pressure receptors, 75 cold and 13 heat receptors. The skin can also detect even the very slightest vibration.18 It interprets and digitizes our outer world into a series of impulses which our inner selves can understand clearly.

The skin is piezoelectric and when it is vibrated or rubbed it generates electric signals and scalar waves. Our skin is our primary sensory organ. It discriminates between all kinds of energy inputs from light, to sound,

16 Psychic Discoveries Behind the Iron Curtain, by Sheila Ostrander and Lynn Schroeder, Prentice-Hall, 1970, pages 170-185.
17 "The Skin, Our Fifth Sense", Explore More Magazine, March/April 1996.
18 Ibid.

to heat, to electricity, and many other forms of energy. These inputs are then interpreted though both the nervous system and the acupuncture channels and transduced or transformed into signals which are then transferred through these networks and decoded by the brain. The Neurophone® injects its signal utilizing the brain's code. Flanagan described the skin as a receptor in the following way:

"Our skin is not just a covering; it is an enormously sensitive organ with hundreds of thousands of receptors for temperature and brotactile input. Every organ of perception develops ontologically and phylogenetically out of skin. In the embryo skin folds and then forms our eyes and ears. Our skin may contain the latent capacity to perceive light and sound. I think by stimulating the skin with energy."[19]

When the Neurophone® was first developed, scientists who study nerve physiology believed that the brain was hard-wired to various nerves and nerve bundles. These neurophysiologists believed that the brain was only able to perform sensory functions through definable linear channels. These scientists believed that the input could only be received, converted and sent through these nerve pathways. In this belief they concluded that sound could only be interpreted by the brain if it was transmitted through the eighth cranial nerve which runs from the inner ear to the brain. Today, however, more and more scientists accept the theory of the holographic brain – the brain as a three dimensional computer which can translate data into understandable patterns. What this means is that if the coding system were understood and the input signal were properly formed, any effect which could be patterned in the brain could be recreated outside of it and projected inward through alternative channels. If the body is viewed as an antenna, then the skin can be viewed as the receiving energy converter, the transducer, the transformer or the

19 Mega Brain Power; Transform your life with mind machines and nutrients, by Michael Hutchison, ISBN 1-56282-770-7, 1994. pg. 111.

shifter of the energy into a new form which can be moved through the body to the brain. Theoretically, we should be able to hear and see through numerous channels.

The brain has a holographic system which is what gives the human mind the ability to hold such huge amounts of data. We are a huge impulse of modulating, undulating energy through which data is transferred. The discovery of the neuro code and transmitting system is the most profound aspect of this invention.

According to Flanagan, *"The key to the Neurophone®️ is the stimulation of the nerves of the skin with a digitally encoded signal that carries the same timing ratio encoding that is recognized as sound by any nerve in the body."* Thus the impulse is converted to understandable sound. He went on to say; *"All commercial digital speech recognition circuitry is based on so-called dominant frequency power analysis. While speech can be recognized by such a circuit, the truth is that speech encoding is based on time ratios. If the frequency power analysis circuits are not phased properly, they will not work. The intelligence is carried by phased information. The frequency content of the voice gives our voice a certain quality, but frequency does not contain inform-ation. All attempts at computer voice recognition and generation are only partially successful."* What this means is that Flanagan created a system where a more complete preservation of data was achieved. For sound recording, this system would provide the ultimate sound system. By understanding timing ratios the basic language of humans could be broken down and electronically synthesized.

The spoken words, ideas and definitions of words could be compressed by a computer and transferred to the brain at a very high level without brain filtered distortion. The input is direct and memory effects are long term. The rate at which the brain can take information in is significantly higher than recorded sound or visual inputs. To bypass natural filters for long term memory is an incredible attribute of this invention.

During the dolphin research, a method of converting sound to a wave form which could be transmitted thousands of miles was found. The transmission could be realized using minimal energy inputs or, in Flanagan's words, "we could transmit clear voice data through extremely narrow bandwidths. In one device, we developed a radio transmitter that had a bandwidth of only 300 hertz while maintaining crystal clear transmission. Since signal-to-noise ratio is based on bandwidths considerations, we were able to transmit clear voice over thousands of miles."

The prototype of the newest generation of the Neurophone® has been developed and is being released for sale at the same time as the release of this book. The Neurophone® is a brain biofeedback device and signal processor for bioenergetic-computing and imaging. The system will deliver information with state-of-the-art digital processing and be capable of formatting any input signal or any sound or compressed sound input signals. The sound quality varies from person to person with initial use. The quality in terms of volume and clarity improves over the first weeks use to its individually dependent level of efficiency.

What else does it do?

It was also discovered that the Neurophone® could be used to "entrain the brain". In other words, the device could be made to create a signal which would cause the brain to synchronize itself with the signal being generated by the external driver or signal generator. By creating the right frequency in the brain certain states of consciousness can be manipulated. There are dozens of devices and systems on the market which can create these effects at some level. However, the Neurophone® presents the ultimate in whole brain entrainment possibilities. A complete system for learning can be developed by the listener which is tailored to meet his needs. Tape recorded information can be fed through the Neurophone® for imprinting on the mind. As a memory tool the invention is far superior to anything else available.

It has been reported that the Neurophone® could be useful for initiating behavioral changes in people. Dr. Eldon Taylor worked as a specialist for Salt Lake City law enforcement in forensic hypnosis. He founded Progressive Awareness Research, Inc., and was permitted to run experiments in subliminal behavior modification in the Utah State Prison system. Subliminal behavior modification involves the use of messages which can not be heard consciously. What he discovered about the Neurophone® was that when he turned the sound of the device down below the level of hearing it was extremely effective. Dr. Taylor said, "In every instance in which we employed the Neurophone® at subthreshold levels, the message was acted upon more consistently than when any type of audible communication, including hypnosis, was employed."[20]

During the research on dolphins discussed elsewhere in this book, a test was conducted called "The Beat Frequency Test". It was well known that sound waves of two slightly different frequencies create a "beat" note as the waves cancel each other out. For example, if a sound of 17,000 hertz is played into one ear at the same time as a sound of 17,030 hertz is played into the other ear, a beat note of 30 hertz is perceived. This mechanical sound cancellation takes place in the bone structure of the inner ear. There is another beat phenomena which is known as binaural beat. In this phenomena the same principal holds true except the beat frequency appears in the middle of the brain therein "entraining the brain" to pulse in rhythm to the beat. What this means is that the brain is harmonized with the induced frequency. This was first recognized and applied to the reaching of altered states of consciousness by Robert Monroe of the Monroe Institute in Virginia.[21]

20 Super-Memory; The Revolution, by Sheila Ostrander and Lynn Schroeder, ISBN 0-88184-691-0, 1991, pages. 62-65.
21 The Monroe Institute, Route 1, Box 175, Fabar, Virginia 22938.

The Neurophone® can alter states of consciousness. These states could be programed in through the Neurophone®. In the dolphin research it was verified that the sound being delivered through the Neurophone® was not the result of bone conduction or the same as a binaural beat like Monroe's. It was something much different. It was a complete nervous system vibration or beat which caused sound information to bypass the normal "filters" or internal mechanisms which otherwise interfere with our ability to communicate with our brains and learn and retrieve information.

The use of the Neurophone® for learning and recall is an important attribute and, perhaps one of the principle uses of the device. It is known that the brain retains all knowledge that it receives, even the obscure kind of knowledge we do not consciously focus on. This has been demonstrated when people are placed under hypnosis and are able to recall the names of all the books on a shelf or the number of telephone poles on the way home from work. The information is all there – the problem centers on the retrieval system of the mind. The Neurophone® allows for the programing and recall of information by by-passing these filters. The Neurophone® it is theorized, might also be establishing new thought pathways that, once opened, remain accessible to people. This would explain how the long term memory effect might actually work.

In the most recent research into the possibilities of this technology, Patrick and his wife, Gael Crystal Flanagan, have developed other modes of Neurophonic transmission. They have also developed a way of reversing the circuit so that they can detect scalar energy waves generated by living systems. Being able to receive the full signal would allow for altering the signal and for producing sequenced sound vibrations which have the greatest positive effects on the scalar energy patterns. A system could be designed which would allow for the manipulation of growth and control of disease in plants. In humans many disorders are mediated and controlled by the brain. The brain transfers the energy which may take the form of a disease or other physiological disorder. Restoring the flow of energy in many ways can provide relief from pain, increased creativity and learning. What are the possibilities? Can information be compressed through optical or electrical mediums for thought transference? Could a system be developed for whole communications at a distance - electronic telepathy?

Other anomalous effects created and discovered with the Neurophone® included a form of thought transference between people. The area of mental telepathy between people was highly controversial in the early 1960's and 1970's. Today, there have been sufficient experimental trials to prove that telepathy is real. What has hitherto not been shown is the mechanism by which the actual telepathic effect occurs. By reversing the design of the Neurophone® so that it acts as a signal pickup and broadcast system in conjunction with another unit serving as a receiver, a system for information exchange can take place.

Another observation made by Flanagan was that when the device was in use it stepped up the body's energy fields in such a way as to effect photographic film. The energy field surrounding the body would show up on film. This was discovered one day while Flanagan was in his dark room developing film while listening to the Neurophone®. What he saw was that when the Neurophone® was on and he touched the undeveloped film he caused an exposure of the film. The stepped up energy which was coming from his body could be clearly seen on the developed film. He experimented with this effect at some length and discovered the same kind of energy halos in all living things which were tested.

In these tests he also found that the energy patterns changed with changes in the skin dielectric. What this means is that with changes in diet, mood, emotion or other mental states the energy would change or shift.

Research into this phenomena led Flanagan to the Soviet electrician Semyon Davidovich Kirlian, who had discovered the body energy halo effect in 1939, capturing the energy image on film and naming the new photographic process Kirlian Photography. The Kirlian effect created by a high frequency oscillator has become relatively well known in recent years. What happens when living tissue is stimulated by the high frequency generator is an amplification of vibration which can then be captured on film. The vibrational level of this energy level is otherwise not perceptible to the eyes as they do not resonate at these frequencies and consequently the eyes can not be tuned to see the energy which surrounds living things. These subtle energies are the energies of the future of science. The detection devices were not well understood and still remain somewhat of a mystery for most scientists even though the cause and effect relationships are well documented. Devices to create Kirlian photographs can be obtained for less then $500.00 and can be constructed for even less. The idea that this kind of imaging could be enhanced with Neurophonic technology is interesting. Even more interesting is the possibility of using the brain, an electrically mediated organ, to send signals which could be artificially shaped to create specific desired effects in the human body beyond Neurophonic hearing. Increased levels of research into the control and manipulation of human energy could lead to significant breakthroughs in mental and physical health. The idea that individuals could gain significant levels of control over their own mental functions and the effects of those functions is profound. The brain is the reality mediator for each individual and it can be artificially tuned for increased information collection and, perhaps, other effects.

What was found through direct measurement were a number of electrical effects related to diet and external inputs to the body. A correlation was drawn between the acupuncture points and the energy levels present at the surface of the skin. In one test the dielectric skin constant was measured and found to vary over a wide range depending on emotional state. It was also found that it could be altered significantly by ingesting raw amino acids. Flanagan found that consuming one ounce of pure amino acids altered his body's capacitance from 100 picofarads to .01 microfarads in three minutes.

In another measuring test he found that skin resistance varied over the human body and that the point of high energy could be isolated using electrodes and a signal amplifier. These high energy points corresponded to the acupuncture points in the human body. The acupuncture points do not line up exactly with nerve bundles. The acupuncture points do, however,line up with the energy field grid points on the human body, all of which can be correlated with points charted thousands of years ago by the Chinese. In a recent trip to Europe to visit my close friend, research scientist Dr. Reijo Makela, I was introduced to a healing method which utilizes some of these principles.

In the last twelve years Dr. Makela has treated over 12,000 patients through a holistic energy and nutrition system. On my visit, Reijo demonstrated his sensing device which is used for locating the acupuncture points on the human body. He then used a device which caused a high frequency electrical signal, in conjunction with a helium neon laser, to impulse through the acupuncture points in order to balance human energy. Using this method the acupuncture treatment was significantly more effective than the system which employed only needles. The system offered precision location of the points and assured energy delivery and balance. The success Dr. Makela has had with this system has been profound. He has caused reversals in medical conditions which were otherwise considered untreatable. He has treated a wide variety of illnesses. As a result of his efforts over 600 past patients created two supporting foundations in Europe to promote his work.

Recently I had an opportunity to introduce Dr. Flanagan and Dr. Makela. I believe they have experiences and skills which will eventually lead to significantly improved treatment and diagnostic equipment. When I returned from Europe I brought back a device used in the Makela healing system. This compact signal generator first locates the acupuncture point using the electrode as a probe to measure differences in skin resistance. Once the energy point is located the device beeps or a light flashes indicating correct placement of the electrode. A switch on the electrical box is then thrown and the device converts from a probe to a signal generator. The device then sends a precisely shaped wave form, at just the right frequency, voltage and amperage to cause the acupuncture channel to energize. This device is being re-engineered by Dr. Flanagan in order to make it available to the public as a low cost biofeedback and individual energy balancing system. When this work is completed it will be jointly brought forward by Makela, Flanagan and myself.

The Brain

By the time we reach adulthood the human brain has developed more than 100 billion neurons. These neurons create connections with others, creating over 100 trillion circuits. These connections represent more than the number of galaxies in the known universe. These connections create the potentials of the human brain. The way information flows into the brain in the establishment of these connections is relevant to our understanding of some of the underlying possibilities in the brain.

It was believed that the connections were the outgrowth of genetic patterning. It was believed that the wiring of the brain was set in the genes. There are 50,000 genes involved in the formation of the central nervous system, which is not enough to account for the complex patterns of brain circuits. The complexity requires more input, more sources for creation of these complexities. Some have now suggested that the outer world – the environment, through its innumerable inputs, is what actually form these complex connections. In other words, the interactions we experience outside of ourselves form the basis of who we are. Perceptions on many levels are possible through these networks and no two persons are wired the same.22

According to developmental neurobiologist Carla Shatz of the University of California, Berkeley, the brain stays malleable where these connections can occur. For instance the research she cites suggests that sensory areas (touch, sight, sound, etc.) develop in early childhood. The emotional limbic system is wired by the time children reach physical maturity and the capacity to build understanding continues to take form until about age sixteen.23

We also know that sensory development as it relates to touch occur very early in life for example, the handling of infants is critical to their development. The sense of touch and the development of connectedness to others is well known. Children are much calmer and more secure when handled often by loving adults.24

Incredible educational potentials exist if we load our experience with the kind of situations which build our capacities. If we introduce the right learning possibilities and experiential mixes with the proper brain development, a good deal more would be possible in terms of education. At the same time, we need to recognize that some of the problems which manifest in people, whether sensory, emotional or intellectual are very difficult to cure.

The issue of hard wiring is important to understanding where this is all headed. Hard wiring of brain circuitry is important because if the wiring could not be changed then many of our mental limits would be locked into place. Two approaches are being taken to effect the way the brain processes information. Some are

21 Your Child's Brain" by Sharon Begley, <u>Newsweek</u>, February 19, 1996, pages 55-62.
23 Ibid.
24 "The Skin, Our Fifth Sense", <u>Explore More Magazine</u>, March/April 1996.

using chemical means to change the way the circuits in the brain handle the data. Other systems are electromechanical and are showing increased potentials.

The Neurophone® technology bypasses wired neurocircuits and gets the information into the brain while stimulating new neuro connections and creating new pathways. These new pathways offer an opportunity to revitalize dormant portions of the brain by stimulating them to activity and by increasing connections. It appears from reports of early users of the Neurophone® that this is exactly what was occurring.

Researcher Patricia Kuhl of the University of Washington, reported that by six months of age infants have already formed auditory maps for sound information to flow through the brain. Through her studies she concluded that the wiring is not only different between children who have been raised hearing different languages but also that they are "functionally deaf" to sounds which are not part of their native tongue. The mind map for auditory input is completed by the child's first year. What this means is that the other neurons available for learning other languages by age ten are no longer forming new connections, making it highly unlikely that a person will acquire other languages at the proficiency of natives when learning them later in life.[25] The Neurophone® offers a new way to forge these connections and increase potentials far beyond what might otherwise be possible.

Without a way to change the information input pathways – a tool to open new webs of circuitry – new information, valuable for human growth and expansion, is not possible. The Neurophone® capitalizes on ancient genetic matrixes where new information can be fed to the brain. The "window" periods where learning can take place can be reopened for new inflows of data. The observations of users confirms this potential.

---

25 'Your Child's Brain" by Sharon Begley, <u>Newsweek</u>, February 19, 1996, pages 55-62.

The Neurophone® was used by some women while pregnant. The sound information was transferred into both the mother and child's neuronetworks with profound effects. These individuals reported children who were well advanced in their intellectual development. These children had opportunities to take in undistorted sound information even before the sensory organs developed. Before they had ears they had neuropathways being created via the Neurophone®.

The Neurophone® may offer more than new hearing technologies for those who do not have the ability to hear. It perhaps has greater implications for all of us interested in developing our higher learning potentials.

My family has been active in Alaskan educational issues for over 40 years. Both of my parents were educators and I was past President of the Anchorage Council of Education/AFT and the Anchorage Council of Education. I also chaired a committee in Alaska which explored the possibilities for greater choice in education here in Alaska. As an educational leader I always found the disconnect between new technologies and education to be huge. These separations are pushing us backward at a time when the need for increasing information capacity and retention is greater that it has ever been. My own migration from politics and education to research, writing and science was a shift needed in order to bring these kinds of technologies forward. The information revolution is the wave we have chosen to ride and the Flanagan Neurophone® represents the best technology yet brought forward.

Chapter 4

Life Energy

Mainstream scientists recognize five sensing systems that the body uses to transform physical energy into information. These systems include our senses of smell, hearing, taste, touch and sight. Our nervous system transforms external stimuli into digital electromagnetic signals which our body then reacts to.

In order to survive, all living organisms must maintain a high energy state in relation to their environment. If living things reach equilibrium with the environment they die. Every time we think a thought, twitch a muscle or move we expend some of our vital energy. In order to prevent ourselves from reaching a state of equilibrium we require the continual flow of free energy (negative entropy). The struggle for existence depends on how well equipped each organism is for capturing available energy. Energy is continually flowing through every living thing, entering the system at a high energy state and leaving in a degraded state as some energy is absorbed. All organisms survive by being able to accumulate free energy from their environment.

We exchange both matter and energy with our environment in the process of life. We maintain ourselves far from energy equilibrium with the environment by continuing to feed from available energy all around us. In living systems smooth, free energy flow is of primary concern in order to maintain the highest vitality and health.

The quality of the bioenergy we take into our system is also of great importance. If the energy being added to the living organism is harmonious, then vitality is increased while disharmonious energy inputs create stress and ill health. All living things try to maintain inner balance. If the energy coming into the organism creates imbalance, then the living system immediately sets out to compensate and create balance. This rebalancing burns vital energy. For instance, the continual bombardment of living things with man-created electromagnetic, air, and water pollutants wastes vital energy and increases stress.

Stress is universally recognized as the number one killer of living organisms, including humans. As our technology increases, we continue to add stressors to our environment which ultimately impact us in negative ways. Recognition of these stressors is the foundation of preventative electromagnetic medicine. Through the introduction of balancing technologies and the reduction of created stress, general health can be improved. Some of the factors which contribute to stress, include electromagnetic pollution, plastic based clothing, acoustic or sound pollution, emotional stress, positive ions, improper diet, improper architectural design of our homes, and drugs. Individual stressors do not create major energy drains, however, the cumulative effect of all of the factors of stress we encounter throughout long periods of time do impact us significantly. The cumulative effect results in chaotic life energies which eventually leads to death.

Removing the Stress

Several things can be done to improve overall body balance and remove stress. Pure water which is not treated by chemicals is easy to obtain and adds a great deal to overall health. Water packaged in plastic bottles should be avoided and glass containers utilized whenever possible. The energy available in pure water can be enhanced by simply putting the container in the sun. It can also be improved using some of the technologies described elsewhere in this book.

Clothing has a significant effect on a person's

stress level. By simply altering what we wear we can increase our energy vitality. All artificial clothing develops a high voltage negative electrostatic field which destroys the body's natural electric field balance and attracts air-borne pollutants to the wearer. Air-borne pollutants are positively charged and are attracted to negatively charged objects. Additionally, artificial fabrics are impregnated with poisonous chemical fire retardants and plastic based clothing does not allow the skin to breathe. Plastics hold in moisture and provide a place for bacteria and funguses to grow.

Natural fibers radiate a positive field which reinforces the bioelectric field of the human body. The positive charge attracts negative ions to the wearer which is what causes the re-enforcment effect. Also, natural fibers do not retain moisture; instead they allow the skin to breathe. When choosing clothing be careful to select those made of natural fabrics like cotton, silk, linen, and wool. Acetates, orlons, nylons and polyesters are examples of plastic-based fabrics which should be avoided.

Where We Live Matters

The place where we choose to live can have a profound effect on our health and consciousness. The ancient art of choosing sites for homes and temples is known in China as Geomancy.

The earth is a living organism which can be equated to the human body. The earth has streams and rivers whereas man has blood vessels and acupuncture meridians.The earth has minerals and rocks while humans have bones and sinews. The earth has trees and people have hair covering their bodies. The earth has an outer skin and man has a protective skin. The earth has the sun and man has his heart.

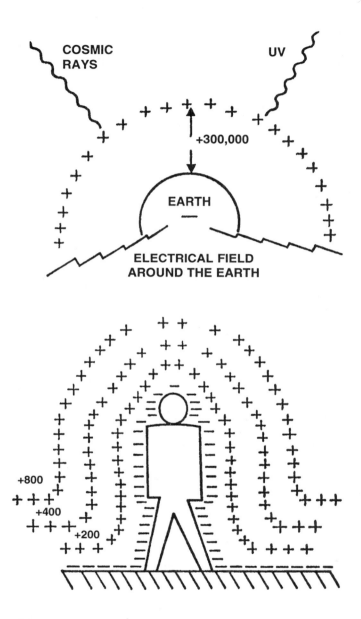

Distortion of Earth's field around the body of a man, note similarty to the fields described as auras.

By understanding our own energies we can begin to understand how mankind has made the earth sick by poor placement of cities. The energy systems of the earth are in a great state of imbalance and it will, like the human body, find ways to rebalance itself. These are the laws of science and nature.

When we find an energy point location where we wish to live, we need to consider the structure of the place to be built. Energy points are where natural lines of energy intersect. Some of these correspond to the locations of ancient temples and structures. The primary points have been laid out in grids by Russian researchers and others. The energies in these locations are those generated by the natural processes of the earth. These energies resonate at a predominant frequency of 7.83 hertz, known as Schumann's Resonance.

The geometric structure of our dwelling and its dimensional unit of measure are of utmost importance. According to Flanagan, the life energy wavelength corresponds to the Hebrew Sacred Cubit (HC) of 25 U.S. inches. Use of this unit of measure in constructing our homes will add to our overall wellbeing.[26, 27] This is the measurement unit believed to have been used in the construction of the Great Pyramid of Giza, Egypt. The base of the Great Pyramid measures 9131 inches which when divided by 25 inches equals 365.24 which is the number of days in an earth year. Cubits and harmonics should be used in architecture. The smallest fraction of a cubit used in construction should be one fourth or 6.25 inches. The internal and external measurements should be within a two percent tolerance.

Other considerations when constructing dwellings should include the proportions described in the chapter of this book called "Pyramids, Geometrics and Energy". Construction should also include careful selection of the

26 <u>Sacred Geometry</u>, by Robert Lawlor, Thames and Hudson 1982, ISBN 0-500-81030-3.
27 <u>How to Triple Your Energy</u>, by Dr. Patrick Flanagan, a seminar summary from 1981.

building materials to avoid those which create hazards such as fiberglass and other synthetics.

Violating the Rules

Dr. Ilya Prigogine of Belgium received the Nobel Prize in 1978 for discovering that the Second Law of Thermodynamics can be reversed. This law states that all energy systems are running down, moving from a structured state to chaos, from concentration to dilution, from free energy to bound energy or from usable to unusable energy. In other words, this law implies that the universe and all life will eventually run down. Dr. Prigogine found that under certain conditions entropy (the amount of usable energy) can be reversed creating negentropy or negative entropy. These conditions show that systems are not closed but are openly exchanging matter and energy with the environment.

When a living organism takes in energy, it uses part of it and discards the rest as waste. If the organism were able to increase its energy through-put it would reverse entropy and grow younger. Proper exercise is one of the ways to increase energy flow through the living system and, to some degree, reverse entropy. As a person increases his metabolism (use of energy) he compensates by eating more calories. As the person burns more energy he does not gain weight. Instead, the excess free energy reverses the entropy of the living system. There are a number of exercises that increase the energy of the body.

Chapter 5

Talking With the Animals

When Flanagan was 20 he was invited to join a very special research project for the United States Navy: The Dolphin Communication Project, was a program funded in the 1960's by the Navy in order to determine if a system of communication could be established with dolphins.

Dr. Dwight Wayne Batteau, the head of the project and a professor of physics and mechanical engineering at Tufts and Harvard University had heard about Flanagan's uncanny abilities with computers and electronics. He sought out Flanagan and made him part of the research team. Flanagan became Vice President of Listening Incorporated, a Massachusetts corporation.

The objective of the project was to develop a system for converting dolphin speech into human speech and then translating human speech into dolphin speech.

There were two research centers for the project. One in Arlington, Massachusetts, outside of Boston, where the equipment and hardware for the project was developed and constructed. The second research center was in a closed off lagoon located on a small island in Hawaii called Coconut Island where the dolphins were located and the actual tests performed.

During the course of the work a 30 word vocabulary was established with the dolphins. The project also demonstrated that dolphins could think conceptually.

During the course of the work Dr. Batteau, the principal person on the research project, died and the project began to falter. One of the other consultants on the project was the noted psychologist B.F. Skinner who held the view that animals could not think conceptually, and his conclusions caused the project to be foolishly scuttled. Skinner believed that animals could not follow a series of instructions, one sequenced after another. He believed that the animal being so instructed would forget the first direction in a sequence and only perform the last one given. However, by the time the project group had established the 30 word vocabulary the team could instruct the dolphin to go out and touch a ball, turn left, go through some hoops and then return to the starting point. The dolphins could perform the assigned tasks after only being given the instructions once. The team tried various combinations of activities with these wonderful creatures and in all instances where the instructions were given they were followed precisely. This demonstrated reasoning and thinking skills that were not thought possible for animals.

Surprisingly enough, the team also discovered that dolphins learned at a more rapid rate than most humans. The scientists believed that if they could reach a vocabulary of around 300 words they could communicate complete abstract thoughts with the dolphins.

Patrick maintains to this day that this work should have continued. He believes that had this research gone forward it could have led to breakthroughs in knowledge of great value to mankind while at the same time increasing the empathy of humans to the condition of some of Earth's other creatures.

Dolphin brains are unique in that the side lobes which control abstract and creative thoughts are substantially larger than that of humans. Why is this relevant? When comparisons are made between man and monkeys it is inevitably pointed out that man has large side lobes and monkeys have none which is what distinguishes thinking humans from instinctual animals. This of course raises the question which the egos of most of us are unwilling to contemplate...is it possible that dolphins might have greater creative capacity than humans and are only limited by their physical form from actualizing these potentials?

Dolphins can perceive location, size and the nature of objects by sound reflection more efficiently than we can perceive using our eyes. In addition, their eyesight is better than ours with the standard for dolphins being 20/10 as opposed to 20/10 for humans. They also have a form of telescopic sight; they can actually pull objects into closer view. Under or above water they can see at great distance and in strong detail.

It was during the dolphin project that Flanagan and the team developed the basis for many new technologies. They were able to isolate the actual encoding system used by the brain to interpret speech. They were also able to figure out the way the brain worked in locating sound sources in three dimensional space.

These discoveries provided the basis for the development of a three dimensional holographic sound recording and projection system. This system enabled the recording of sound in such a way that it could be projected out through a set of speakers and into a room so that listeners thought the sound was appearing out of thin air, like throwing the sound into a point out in front of the listener and then having it bounce back so it seemed to the listener that the sound just appeared in a space in front of the listener.

This technology allowed the team to locate whales in the open sea by listening to their whistles over vast distances and then to pinpoint their location.

They discovered, the human outer ear functions as a phase encoding array which generates a time-ratio code that is used by the brain to locate the source of sounds in three dimensional space. For example, the shape of the ear is not just a chance happening but actually contributes to the ability of the brain to translate and locate sound. Try this: Close your eyes and have someone make noises in various parts of the room. With a little practice you can accurately locate the direction and location of the sound. When the outer ear is bent or distorted this ability is significantly reduced or eliminated entirely.

Another way to demonstrate this effect is to think about a noisy party where you are still able to locate the source of various sounds and voices while filtering out the others. An ordinary microphone can not isolate the source of sounds which is why in most embassies or areas where sensitive conversations might take place the security organizations use what are called "hard rooms." These rooms have hard wooden floors and hard surfaces which, if bugged, will pick up the echoes of voices in such a way as to totally distort the conversations. The placement of a model of a human ear over the microphone itself was found to totally clarify the sound and eliminate the echo effect making a hard room useless.

In the underwater work with dolphins the team used 18 inch metal ears attached to hydrophones to pinpoint the specific location of the creatures. In water sound travels about five times faster than in air so the ears were made larger in order to maintain the timing ratios that the human brain uses to locate objects in our natural environments. The team also made large plastic ears which were used during the Vietnam War. These ears were the same proportions as real ears but were much larger. They provided a way of hearing distant sounds and isolating their source location in the middle of the jungle with a high degree of accuracy. It was found that humans could adapt to ears of almost any size because sound recognition is based on a time-ratio code. The timing code is the key to the sound transfer.

The team was also able to reverse this concept,

establishing a way to project sound so that it was perceived as coming from some specific point in space rather than from a loudspeaker. This particular technology would allow for the recording of sound in such a way as to make it seem as if you were at a live concert rather than listening to a recording. This technology was used only once for this purpose when Flanagan allowed the Beach Boys to record one of their albums with a special set of laser microphones he had developed.

The Neurophone® was used in the dolphin research as well. This device allowed humans to perceive sounds otherwise far outside of the range of human hearing. Some of these dolphin sounds are vibrated at the frequency of 250,000 cycles per second where the human hearing upper limit is more on the order of 16,000 to 20,000 cycles per second. The technology, which was in part derived from the dolphin project, led to the development of the newest prototype, the digital Neurophone®.

Chapter 6

Hearing the Sound of One Hand Clapping

Listening Incorporated was the place Patrick Flanagan found himself in the mid-1960's. It was here that his work with dolphins and advanced information and communication systems took place. The annual report to stockholders issued December 19, 1966 was, in part, written by Flanagan and served as a summary of his early work.

In this annual report a vivid picture is painted in our minds by the words of the author: *"Imagine sitting by the seashore and listening to the waves. If you can, now imagine that the sound of waves along the shore are talking to you. The sound might say, 'In front of you is a sandy, sloping beach, but far over to the right is an outcropping of rock, and there is a quiet cove on the left.' And you might also imagine that, whatever the weather, the waves speak of those same features. One time in a loud, wild voice, another time in a soft, gentle voice, but always of the same shore."*

The author continued, *"Now can you imagine wind in a forest, and the sounds tell of leaves and branches, of large and small trees, and of the brush and forest floor. The sound from the floor is a quiet sound, the trunks of the trees are columns of whispers, and the leaves are a flutter and rustle of sound. Again, no matter the weather, whether rain or wind, the sounds tell of the same forest, and the voices may change but the message is the same except as the seasons change the character of features of which the whispers comment."*

"These are not merely romantic imaginings; they are facts for the observing. Doesn't your kitchen sound like your kitchen, and your living room sound like your living room? Isn't the office of one character to be heard and the neighborhood bar another? Not by reason of the sounds of voices, footsteps, and movement alone, but by reason of what the rooms do to the sounds which fill them. Movie sound men have been aware of this for decades, and always tape silence on the set, for dubbing if necessary.Inescapably, each feature of our environment modifies the sound of nature in its own way, which we may hear, if we listen."

"Now think of the human vocal tract as a room of mobile walls, and that the shape and substance of the room can be heard when filled with sound. And this whether by whisper, shout, or song. Or by a buzzer, a belch, or an electronic reproduction of a train. Isn't it clear that the particular sound is of lesser importance than what the structure does to the sound? We may say that sound is transformed by the vocal tract, and that the resultant sound carries the marks of having been there."

"Consider that sound is transformed by its environment, then if it were possible to create an inverse to the environmental transformation, we would have a picture of that environment. We at Listening are learning how to do this."

"We are rapidly becoming expert at information, communication, and knowledge in the recognition and synthesis of acoustical signals and environmental characteristics."

In the pages of the report which followed were summaries of the various technologies which the research team at Listening Incorporated was working on. The projects are each briefly described in the report.

Dolphin Communications Program

This project was undertaken through a contract with the United States Naval Ordnance Test Station in China Lake, California. Under the contract the group had created a system where 18 words could be translated. As the project continued into the early part of the following year the vocabulary had increased to 30 words.

This project was designed to begin a program of human to dolphin communication that would be useful in certain military applications. The spin-off of the research was that the coding system for the translation created significant increases in the knowledge of speech and hearing.

Man-Dolphin Translator

Out of the program evolved a translation device which would convert human speech to the whistle sounds normally produced by dolphins. The man-dolphin translator (MDT) was an effective tool for the communications effort and was complemented by the dolphin-man translator (DMT) for converting the whistles of the dolphins to the sounds of human speech. These electronic devices were the backbone of the communications effort.

Sondol, The Sonic Dolphin

When dolphins are in murky water or darkness they use sound echoes for the purpose of positioning and to determine what is in their immediate and distant surroundings.

The team developed a device called a Sondol, and had the opportunity of testing it on human subjects. The device showed potential for use by the blind in sensing their environment and had potential for scuba divers for increasing their perception when in dark or muddy conditions. With a small amount of practice anyone with normal hearing can learn to use this device. After a little practice subjects could find their way around in total visual darkness.

This device would allow a human to work underwater and, with practice, a trained diver could be able to identify specific objects up to three hundred yards away.

Spatial Localization

One of the strangest, and yet the simplest, set of observations led the president of the company, Dr. Dwight Wayne Batteau, to invent the ear. More accurately stated, Dr. Batteau discovered the importance of the specific human ear shape and the vital part the ear itself played in the sound localization process. In other words he discovered how the ear was utilized by the brain to locate the sound source in three dimensional space.

This phenomena of localization was the direct result of the outer ear (the pinna) interacting with incoming sound wave fronts. The brain/computer used the outer ear as a kind of delicate steerable antenna array which would transform the incoming sounds into impulses and direct the sound location information to the brain. There were three main products developed as a result of this discovery. These discoveries were later further improved by Flanagan by combining his own original thinking to the technology.

Air-Ears: These devices consisted of a pair of microphones mounted in molds of human ears and spaced approximately the same distance as would normally be the case on a human head. The result was that the sound recorded from the device was picked up as a binaural beat frequency. Tape recordings of these sound pickups using these special microphones retained the location information. In other words the listener could readily identify the relative position, location, or the originally recorded sound if the recordings were listened to with a set of head phones. A person could close his eyes and it would be as if he had been transported to the location of the original recording, as if he had walked into the concert hall.

The sound depth was incredible. The vertical, horizontal and the distance relationship of the sounds were all perfectly preserved on the taped recording. This was not just the right side left-side of standard stereos - it was holographic sound.

One of the most interesting applications and uses of this device was in recording debates, lectures or conferences where there might be a number of speakers. During these recording events speakers would speak sequentially or at the same time. The use of the Air-ear preserved the location of the speaker on the sound track. In this way a person listening to the recording could focus his attention on the individual of choice and than replay the recording and totally focus on another person just like a person can do in a crowded room with numerous conversations going on at the same time. The sound of each had its own source instead of being jumbled together as is the case with normal recording microphones.

Underwater Ears: At the time of the report the underwater ears were constructed of stainless steel and were 11 inches in size. These ears functioned the same as the air ears but were larger in size to account for the fact that sound travels faster underwater than in air by a factor of five. To accommodate the speed differences of the sound waves the ears had to be larger. Using these ears the listener could locate the source of the sound to within eight degrees. These sounds could also be recorded and preserved for replay later with all of the location properties intact. As with the other device elevation, range and depth could be perceived.

Location Synthesis: This was the outgrowth of the formerly described devices. The idea here was that after gaining the understanding of how the sound was handled by the outer ears a computer could be used to recreate the sound wave or modify it so as to place the sound in any location desired.

Think of a normal intercom in a submarine or even a space ship: you can hear and perhaps identify voices by the sound, but you cannot detect direction. The Location Synthesis device would add that dimension to the intercom. The computer would create and assign initial locations and then the person's movement would become part of an interactive system where spatial relationships would be maintained and projected to others in the craft.

Phoneme Detector

A system of speech recognition was necessary for the Man-Dolphin Translator. As a result, the Phoneme Detector which would recognize various "marks" or specific characteristics of voice generated sounds was devised. This detector when combined with other devices used in the project allowed for a very efficient system whereby machines could be controlled by voice commands.

This system would provide the means for increasingly complex commands to be understood by machines as the language programs could be developed. The specific discoveries related to the time-ratio coding of sound and the subsequent decoding by the brain allowed for this breakthrough. To this day in 1996, a system of voice recognition for complex machine tasking has yet to be produced. Yet, in 1966 the basic technology was discovered with the only real missing link being computing power. Rolling back to the 60's and coupling this discovery with modern computing and electronics will lead to a very sophisticated system of computer-to-human voice interaction.

Square Wave Speech Generator and the Neurophone®

Both of these discoveries were encapsulated in patents filed and held by Patrick Flanagan. These discoveries are the backbone of the holographic sound generating system developed by Patrick and described in much greater detail in other portions of this book. This technological advance, which was built while Patrick was with the company, were the source of both great excitement and deep sorrow. It was with the filing of the patents for the Square Wave Speech Generator that his enthusiasm for the Neurophone® began to wane. It was at this juncture in Flanagan's life that the government took the invention out of his hands for five years under a National Security Order.

Color Sonar and Computer Recognition of Environments

These two other significant inventions were made while Flanagan was with Listening Incorporated. Color sonar was developed by Dr. Batteau. With this system a sonar signal was able to distinguish between objects by taking into account the fact that different materials treat sound waves differently. What this means is that when a signal is sent out over a distance and strikes an object the frequency is slightly altered so that the return signal contains the "signature" of the object. This gives a computer the ability to determine whether an object is a metal submarine or a whale, for example. The frequency differences could then be translated by a computer and put on the sonar screen with color variations based on the return signal frequencies.

The complement to the above discovery was a system for computer recognition of objects. This again, to be most efficient, required substantially more computing power than standard 1966 systems. What was found was that a reflected sound signal carried back all of the characteristics of the objects that the sound was reflected from. What this means is that the returning sound has a picture of the objects it struck contained within it. What this technology was expected to yield was a three dimensional view of objects otherwise invisible under-water.

These two inventions, if combined, would provide a very powerful military and civilian tool of great use today.

Chapter 7

Mountain Air

In the 1970's, while Patrick was working with Listening, Inc. and conducting research at Tufts, he was often consulting on other projects which brought in surplus cash he could use in his work. As a result he was able to regularly make new additions to his home research facilities, evolving a very sophisticated research laboratory. He worked on new ideas continuously and over the years added to his growing list of inventions.

The inventions, he realized, could not all be brought into production at the time of their discovery. The capital requirements for producing all of the inventions would be too large and the markets for the ideas in the 1960's and 1970's were too limited. It seemed that if the ideas were patented, many of the patents would expire before a solid market for the ideas could either be established or the capital acquired to initiate production. As a result, he began to catalog and file the ideas away for future use without applying for patents. The list would grow to over 300 different ideas by 1996.

Flanagan had an unworkable practice of trying to develop dozens of projects at the same time but eventually, he began to keep the focus of his efforts down to less than a dozen projects at a time.

During his early twenties, and after the dolphin project was discontinued, he moved to Los Angeles, California. There he became aware of the significant and increasingly detrimental effects of air pollution on human health. He realized that if the trend continued the long term effects would prove devastating in coming years. In highly polluted cities the particles we inhale can amount to up to two table spoonfuls of these very fine particles daily. The majority of the particles are so fine that they can actually become lodged in the lungs and enter the blood stream causing health problems. These particles include bacteria, viruses, asbestos and other elements. Today, in modern cities, people seem to become sick more often as their immune systems are placed in a continuous state of alert while fighting off the effects of these pollutants and, at the same time, maintaining other normal body defense systems. People with asthma and allergies are being impacted the most as we witness this segment of the population growing at an alarming rate. It is now estimated that around 40% of the population may suffer from respiratory related illnesses or allergies.

Outside air was not the only problem Flanagan observed nearly three decades ago. He found that the problems associated with indoor air might actually be even worse. He observed that smoke, household chemicals, molds, mildews, and the decomposition of house building materials were all contributing to increasingly high levels of pollution. He also observed that the increasing dependence on heating and cooling systems, which recycled the same air, created cumulative effects as the oxygen levels were depleted in inside environments. As Flanagan reached his twentieth year he began to take on the problem as a part of his research efforts at the time.

Indoor air pollution was a bigger problem than most people realized. The pollutants he observed built up because the smallest and most potent pollutants would become positively charged. These particles would remain electrostatically suspended in the air. The larger particles would either settle out as dust or would be filtered out in heating and cooling systems. These problems of indoor air pollution are now recognized by the United States government which, through the Environmental Protection

Agency, has issued warnings about their effects.28

As a consequence of his concern and research, Flanagan developed a design for an incredibly effective air purification technology. This system would provide substantial improvements to the quality of indoor air. The air quality produced with the technology not only would eliminate suspended pollutants and eliminate odors, it would also negatively charge the air and greatly enhance the healthful environment.

Before going much further into the subject of the Flanagan air purifier it really is necessary to define some of the basics. In an atom there are three parts; there are electrons which are negatively charged, there are protons which are positively charged and there are neutrons which have no charge. The protons and neutrons form the nucleus of the atom and the electrons orbit that nucleus. The number of protons are normally equal to the number of electrons which means that the charges they each carry balance or cancel each other out. However, if some of the electrons are pulled out of orbit, then the atom has a positive net charge. Atoms which pull these "freed" electrons into their orbits then have a net negative charge because they contain more electrons than protons. In either case these unbalanced atoms (clusters of atoms) are called ions. Thus ions can be either negative or positive in their electrical charge.

The reason that particles remain electrostatically suspended in the air is because of a phenomena called "space charge". Space charge is caused by an imbalance of ions with most pollutants generating a positive space charge. In order to neutralize this positive space charge it is necessary to inject negative ions into the environment. The negative ions neutralize the space charge of the positively charged particles causing them to precipitate out of the air. These particles will fall out of the air to the ground.

---

28 Environmental Protection Agency Booklet, The Inside Story, A Guide to Indoor Air Quality.

This was the challenge – to create a device that would produce a negative charged ion and inject the ion into the environment. In his private laboratory the independent scientist researched what the Europeans and others were doing to reduce indoor pollutants. Patrick realized that little was being done in this area in the United States and what had been done was not very effective. He designed a powerful ionizer which applied 20,000 negative-volts to an antenna-like needle which would attract positive ions and convert them to negative ions. The results obtained from the device were so effective that several thousand were made and sold prior to gaining a patent.

Flanagan continued to experiment with various ideas surrounding this device. However, in the months which followed he discovered a problem with the new air cleaning unit. The problem was that negative charged particles are attracted to positively charged objects and although the pollutants were charged negatively the walls and drapes were charged positively. This resulted in these objects becoming plated with black soot over several months of operation. The plating impregnated the pores of the paint requiring repainting because it could not be scrubbed off. The soot was literally electroplated into the walls. While a minor setback, a solution to the soot problem would be resolved as the research into the air purification system continued.

Although the Air Purifier remained an important project, he continued to work on others. During the time he was researching the ionizer he was also studying the past works of researchers into anti-gravity. It was during this research that the solution to the blackening soot problem was inadvertently found.

Anti-gravity

In the minds of some scientists the idea of antigravity is beyond fiction. These scientists believe that it is not only within the realm of possibility but that we may be on the threshold of discovering how it can occur. At the same time some are suggesting, based upon anecdotal evidence, that perhaps the Department of Defense may already possess this technology. Flanagan pursued a line of study of certain principles of electricity which earlier researchers had investigated. These investigators had experimented with floating platforms using a little understood "force field" effect.

Flanagan studied the work of Igor Ivan Sikorsky, inventor of the helicopter. Sikorsky also invented a system using electrical energy fed through a wire grid to cause an object to levitate 100 feet into the air. The power source was on the ground. T. Townsend Brown also developed a system for causing levitation effects in small models.

In order to gain their levitation effects, these earlier inventors, Sikorsky and Brown, worked exclusively with direct current (DC) rather that alternating current (AC).[29] Flanagan built and tested the devices of the earlier inventors, however he added to their work by combining the use of a Tesla coil and various capacitors. The capacitors would store up electrical energy releasing it in sequenced bursts of electricity. In duplicating the work of Brown, Flanagan had the advantage of 40 years of advancements in technology. Available to Patrick was a Keithly High-impedance Electrometer which could measure various kinds of energy fields. The electrometer could measure negative ions, electrostatic fields, electric fields and make other energy measurements. Using this device he could take measurements of his various experiments which were not possible to the earlier

[29] Nikola Tesla discovered AC current and the primary uses for it in the late 1880's. He continued to develop his ideas in oscillating currents and resonance effects until the early 1940's. His ideas we continue to take advantage of with the use, in every aspect, of the entire generation, transmission and distribution systems of electrical energy. His other areas of work continue to be highly controversial as many attempt to expand on his ideas and technologies. He also developed the Tesla coil which is used in numerous electrical experiments.

investigators of these strange anti-gravity effects.

What Flanagan observed when using the electrometer was that the greatest force-field manifested itself at the moment the DC power was engaged dropping thereafter to a more regular level. Flanagan concluded from the observation that the effect most likely could be manipulated more efficiently with alternating current (AC). AC current alternates between positive and negative as it cycles back and forth many times per second and gives the effect of always being in a startup mode of operation, keeping the force-field at the highest sustainable level. The new design worked and the force-field increased dramatically.

After finishing his experiment using the electrometer, he reset the device and moved it across the room near his air purification ionizing equipment, inadvertently leaving the electrometer turned on.

Flanagan continued experimenting with his new force-field generator. He was thinking about its operation as he turned the device on and off a few times when out of the corner of his eye he noticed a small movement. The movement was the needle on the electrometer bouncing up and down every time he switched the generator on and off. He couldn't believe what he was seeing and tested it several times with each test result the same. What was so strange to him was that he did not know of any way that the capacitor could be creating negative ions much less be sending them across the room instantly. It was interesting, but there was no time for the inventor to think about this strange phenomena. He had to go back to the breakthrough in the creation of the force field he had just discovered. He was ecstatic. He had made a huge jump in potential levitation technology using alternating current. As he left his work place that evening, his mind racing with new ideas, he left both the coil-capacitor and the electrometer operating.

The next day Flanagan returned to his laboratory

to continue his experiments. When he entered the room he immediately noticed that the usual odors which accompanied his experiments were gone and the room smelled like fresh mountain air. He noticed that the equipment had been left on and somehow had worked as a powerful new kind of air purifier. Like many past inventors this particular discovery was made while investigating other technologies. Out of these levitation experiments came a major step forward in air purification technologies.

Flanagan continued to test the new device by creating different scents and seeing how long it took for the odors to dissipate. His observations in the weeks which followed confirmed that he had indeed found an improved way of purifying air. He also noted that this device did not leave the electroplated black residue of the earlier purification systems.

In testing the device he used a piece of meat left to rot in the sun. He brought the putrid meat into his lab leaving it near the machine. Within a few hours the smell of the meat was gone and in a few days it had dried into beef jerky without leaving an odor behind.

The observations were intriguing and Flanagan continued to work on the ideas intermittently over the next eight years. By 1976, he had finally gained the understanding of the subtle principles behind the unusual effects which made the invention work. It was then that he applied for the first patent on the new technology. Finally he had developed an air purification system without the blackening effect.

The Air We Breathe

The indoor air we breathe builds up increasingly higher positive charges. These positively charged air ions cause a variety of health problems. Positive air ions are also created in great numbers in indoor electric saunas.30 This helps to explain why breathing is hampered and fatigue occurs in this kind of sauna. Conversely, when wood fired steam saunas are used they create negative, healthful, ions. Positive ionization in the environment where we live causes labored breathing and stress. These stresses are eliminated when negative ionization predominates in our living space. Negative ionization enhances our vitality while allowing us to reach greater levels of efficiency and harmony.

In nature, negative ions are produced by a number of forces. Lightning and thunderstorms, the roll of the surf, falling rain drops and the cascade of waterfalls all create negative ions. As do cosmic rays and the interaction of the sun with our environment. The feelings of vitality each of us experience after a thunderstorm or on a walk along the beach are more than an aesthetic impact. It is a biological reaction which begins with an ionic energy exchange. It is the exchange which energizes us with the healthful effects of negative ionization. Negative ions, when introduced into a living space, are magnetically attracted to positive charged sub-microscopic particles. These particles begin clumping together until their weight is so great they fall to the ground.

Positively charged oxygen is difficult for the body to absorb which is why breathing is hampered. Negatively charged oxygen on the other hand increases oxygen uptake into the body by anywhere from 30% to 50%. This increase in capacity has many positive effects including increased lung capacity and overall stress reduction.

The long winters in Alaska and other northern regions cause people to stay indoors most of the time.

30 November 1994 conversations with Dr. Reijo Makela in Finland regarding the negative health effects of saunas based upon their construction. This conversation with Dr. Makela was in the context of a more comprehensive dialog dealing with the health effects of electromagnetic radiations. Dr. Makela is a medical doctor and electrophysiologist.

The positively charged interior environments cause lethargy, depression, irritability and stress. Seasonal Attitude Disorder (SAD) is caused by imbalances in the brain, the results of low light levels coupled with positively ionized oxygen from indoor living. Forced air heating, electric baseboard heating and electric saunas all increase positively charged environments leading to winter depression.

There are reports of the effects of a full moon on people which we have all read about from time-to-time. It has been shown statistically that there are higher crime rates, accidents and other effects from the full moon. It is interesting to note that the highest positive ion count occurs during the full moon. This happens as a result of the relationship between the polarized sunlight reflected from the full moon and the energy state of the earth coupled with interaction between the ionosphere and these bodies. These energy interactions result in physiological and psychological changes in people.

It took eight years for Flanagan to figure out why his technology worked. During this time he developed his theory until he had a clear understanding of how the invention worked and then applied for his first patent which was awarded in the relatively short period of three years.

Flanagan's concluded that the device's effect was caused by a new application of a dielectric field. He concluded that energy could be stored as a dielectric field in what he calls a dielectric stress field. What Flanagan was able to do is affect the dielectric we know as air in a way that caused a cascade of electrons. When Flanagan operated the Tesla coil using standard household current he was able to get up to 100,000 volts with the alternating current switching up to 25,000 times per second. He then sent this power to a set of plates constructed of alternating plates of metal and nonconductive material. The stress built up between the metal plates caused increased levels of stress in the air surrounding the plates, causing the air to release electrons. These electrons do not behave in the same manner as electricity. These electrons travel slower and are referred to as of "intermediate velocity".[31]

What happens as these electrons are knocked loose is that they impact other atoms with sufficient speed to cause those atoms to shed electrons as well. These secondary freed electrons, although slower than the first, are moving at sufficient speeds to impact third sets of atoms causing additional releases of electrons. With each successive release the speed of the electrons slows until they reach the point where they can not continue to cause electrons to be released. In other words, as energy is released the speed of each successive generation of electrons being displaced slows down. As they move slower and slower they are eventually captured by positively charged atoms, pollutants and other surface areas of the room.

The cascading effect of the electrons flowing into the space of a room at various speeds allows for the creation of a negatively charged environment. The neutral particles pick up the negative electrons and turn negative and the positive charged atoms gain a negative electron and become neutral. This is what occurs in nature in rain storms and along the beach.

Another aspect of this negative electron generator is that the electrons will create the same reactions even through solid walls. If the walls are made of dielectric materials, the generator will create stresses on the other side of the wall which in turn will continue the cascading effect of electron release.

---

31 This is a field of energy which is not electric. In order to understand the significance of this we must change our view on nonconductors. Materials that do not allow electricity to flow through them. It was demonstrated by Maxwell, and others, that electrical power could be stored in nonconducting materials like glass in the same way that magnetic energy could be stored in the iron of a magnet. What Flanagan used in this invention was the effect of nonconducting materials which can absorb and hold an energy field.

Flanagan's explanation for how the generator worked also explained how energy is transferred in a thunderstorm. It was thought by scientists that clouds needed to build up energy in a high enough concentration and power level that the energy would eventually leap across the nonconductive air and arc to the ground. What Flanagan demonstrated was that there was another explanation – the electron cascade.

He discovered that air, as a nonconductor within a thunderstorm, builds a dielectric stress field. This field which is impacted by the combination of the built up electric charge and the falling rain creates the cascade of electrons. When the energy pushes the electrons out of their orbits, the air actually acts as a conductor resulting in a flow of negative electricity from the cloud to the earth below in the form of a lighting bolt. In less severe storms, without lightning, the same cascade effect is occurring to a lesser degree.

The Electron Cascade Generator® was the end product of Flanagan's work in this area. It eliminated the blacking soot problem and provided an improved environment. Another advantage of the design is that it eliminates electrostatic induction in the environment. This is very important in electrostatic free environments like computer rooms and electronic assembly areas where a static free environment is essential.

The buildup of energy in our living environments from all heat sources and friction producing machinery increases positive charges. Many of the synthetic materials around us are also positively charged. Cigarettes and smoke carry positive charges. Living within our office buildings and homes, we are increasingly exposed to more positively charged environments which contribute to overall weakened health. The things which we are increasingly adding to our living and work spaces will continue to positively charge our environments. The need to neutralize these charges will continue to increase as our technologies continue to advance. The value of a negatively charged environment in terms of beneficial health effects and human productivity can not be understated. Greater productivity, increased energy, reduced accidents, increased alertness and focused creativity are all beneficial effects caused by the negative charge. In addition, in factory environments where sensitive electronics are used or assembled, this invention reduces the risk of damage, by electrostatic discharges, of electronic components.

Flanagan secured two patents on his technology (see appendix), one in 1978 and the other after ten years of continued research, in 1988. The first patent was improved upon by creating improved dielectric substances. These substances were enhanced by impregnating the plastics used to separate the plates in his devices. These improvements allowed for a significant increase in the effects at substantially lower power requirements. This eventually reduced the level of power needed to run the device to 40 watts.

The concept of the Electron Cascade Generator® may even have applications in areas of the world where outdoor air pollution is a problem. The idea that pollutants could be reduced using systems requiring low amounts of energy in urban areas and may yet be tested. The costs of conducting these tests would be minimal considering their potential benefits.

Chapter 8

The Elixir of Life

Most people think that water is the same everywhere. Not so, say Patrick and Gael Crystal Flanagan. There are significant differences in water throughout the world beyond just the factors which most of us think about – taste, appearance and hardness (mineral content).

The flow of moisture through the world is as important as the flow of blood through the human body. Blood consists of 92% water. The right kind of water is critical to optimum blood flow through the body. It is through the blood circulatory system that toxins are removed and important nutrients delivered to the various parts of our bodies.

Blood carries nutrients to the very fine vessels called capillaries. These in turn release the nutrients into a water-based fluid between the cells called lymph. This fluid surrounds and bathes each cell of our body and keeps each cell from coming into direct contact with others. The capillaries drop oxygen and food into the lymph where it can then be transferred to the cells of our bodies for use. The lymph system requires the right kind of water for it to achieve a maximum level of efficiency.

Dr. Roy Walford of UCLA suggests that our bodies should last 120 years. It has also been suggested that many of the symptoms of the aging process may be due to accumulations of toxins and free-radicals in the cells of the body. These toxins are created by combinations of the food we eat, liquids we drink and air we breathe. The overload of toxins we take into our bodies keeps us from being able to absorb the levels of nutrients we truly need. If the blood we use to transport toxins and nutrients is polluted and thickened, it does not flow as required for optimum health. Research shows that most people have extremely polluted blood streams.

Pure water has a structure which resembles the water found in vegetables and fruits. When the Flanagans observed the juices of freshly picked fruits under high power microscopes, they found "somatids," – thought to be life-energy mediators. "Crystal Energy®" water is uniquely structured to mirror the structure of the water in fruits and vegetables.

The Search For The Ultimate Water

The story of how the Flanagans discovered Crystal Energy® begins several years ago when Patrick was still working for the Huyck Research Laboratories in Connecticut. There he met Dr. Henri Coanda (1885-1972) the father of fluid dynamics. In the 1920's a Rumanian scientist, Dr. Coanda, discovered that water tends to cling to any surface. This discovery was considered so significant by physicists that they called it the "Coanda Effect".

Dr. Coanda was always intrigued by the stories from various parts of the world where people were known to live for extraordinary life spans. He had always thought that it might be connected to the water that they drank. In the early 1930's he journeyed to Hunza, in the Karakorum Mountains just north of Pakistan, where he was told that the secret to the people's longevity was indeed related to the water that they drank. In Hunza people maintain their vitality beyond 100 years.

He was convinced that the structure of the water held the key to its uniqueness. He began considering the molecular structure of the water and measuring samples against ordinary water samples. He studied the crystalline form of water by observing snowflakes manufactured in his laboratory. He found that in the center of each frozen snowflake a small network of tubes of water circulated like blood in the veins of humans or like sap in plants. It was as if the water were alive!

Dr. Coanda observed that when the flow of water slowed and solidified the life of the snowflake ended. It was also observed that when people regularly drank the water which was "alive" it seemed to add life to them. Dr. Coanda continued his research, including analysis of water from several locations where human life spans were extraordinarily long. The same characteristics were observed in the water from these other locations.

Dr. Coanda returned to his native country to become the president of the Rumanian Academy of Sciences. Just prior to leaving he passed on his 60 years of accumulated research to his young colleague and collaborator at Huyck Laboratories, Patrick Flanagan. Coanda told Patrick, "I think you are the only one I know who can eventually come up with a system to make Hunza water available anywhere in the world."[32]

Creating the Ultimate Water

Patrick read everything he could find on water only to conclude that it was one of the world's most mysterious substances. Over the last 15 years Patrick and his wife Gael have focused their research into water's unique properties collecting water samples from around the United States.

Water has a number of unusual attributes. It is considered a universal solvent. It has 36 distinct isotopes, each possessing different properties. It is capable of dissolving any element, even gold. It grows lighter rather than heavier when it freezes. It also has surface tension, a force that causes it to stick to itself, forming a sphere, the shape with the least surface tension and requiring the

---

[32] Secrets of the Soil, Vortex of Life, by Peter Tompkins & Christopher Bird, 1989, Pges 99 -115.

minimum amount of energy to maintain its shape. The potential strength of water is significant. If all of the gas bubbles in water were removed a column one inch think would have the strength of steel.

Water is composed of liquid crystals surrounded by large numbers of chaotically random molecules. It has been theorized that water, even when boiling, contains some crystalline forms which maintain their shape and structure even though the rest of the water is vibrating vigorously at random. As water cools it forms increasing numbers of crystal forms until the entire mass of ice is virtually all crystalline.

When animals, plants and humans drink water they structure the water to form crystals with a smaller number of unorganized molecules. This happens as a result of tiny high-energy particles being suspended in the water. These particles are referred to as colloids and are so small that even powerful microscopes miss them. These small particles act as "energy seeds" which carry a charge causing free molecules of water to become attracted to them thus forming the nuclei of liquid crystals. In order to take this form the colloids must maintain a high electric charge which is possible because of the organic coating they gain in the living system.

Another observation which Flanagan made was that certain crystalline minerals reduce surface tension merely by making contact with these mineral crystals. The reduced surface tension means that the water is "wetter" and more readily absorbed. The observation led to more questions. Where did these mineral crystals gather the energy to change the surface tension of water?

Flanagan found that the surface tension of ordinary tap water was 73 dynes per centimeter while the Hunza water's surface tension was 68 dynes. The Hunza water also maintained a negative net electrical charge which means the rotation of the molecule was to the left rather than the right. The negative charge is one of the key factors in the healthful effects of the water. The negative charge is an important attribute of the water which causes it to bond with positively charged molecules.

The cloudy Hunza water contained virtually every known mineral element including a high concentration of silver. These elements were all in the super-microscopic colloidal form. The water did not contain mineral salts. These tiny particles, the colloids, do not dissolve but remain negatively charged and suspended in the solution as self repelling particles. They are self repelling because the charges are the same and, like the negative poles of two bar magnets, they push away from one another.

The glaciers of Hunza land with their tremendous weight against the surrounding rock formations grind the rock into super-fine powder. This glacial silt is caught up with the melting outflowing water and tumble down the sides of the mountains. The water becomes murky with these suspended solids and even after the movement stops the colloidal minerals remain in the water. These colloidal minerals are coated with some kind of organic substance which he believed came from some ancient strata that the glaciers had also cut through.

In his laboratory, the search for the means to create these same properties in water was attempted. However, he was not able to replicate the characteristics in these early experiments.

Flanagan contemplated the nature of the water and what was happening with it as it flowed down the mountains. He realized that the motion the water experienced might be contributing to the effect. As water travels it flows at different rates of speed causing small spirals or vortices to form. These flows cause an electric current to be generated. This observation made it possible to duplicate this important property in the water.

The water vortices shrink in diameter and extend in length and then contract and enlarge in diameter. The oscillation continues periodically and rhythmically.

The curvature of these vortices mirror a universal matrix observed by other researchers. T.J.J. See, a professor of mathematics, showed that the entire universe revolved around a geometric figure known as a rectangular hyperbola which is the same as a water vortex. This discovery of the basic curve apply to many phenomena according to See, including the laws of magnetism, gravity, planetary motion and, most importantly to the surface-to-volume relationships and the structuring forces which bind all matter. The idea that cosmic energies could be captured and held by the water was pursued by Flanagan in his experiments.

A significant electrical charge is generated by these vortices of water. Flanagan demonstrated the electrical potentials by placing a specially prepared wire down the center of a vortex of water, being careful to not contact the water sides. The water was spinning at about 1,000 revolutions per minute and using another electrode touching the water he was able to record a charge of 10,000 volts.

In the 1930's a German physicist named Paul E. Dobler demonstrated that water flowing in underground passages radiated an unknown energy. This energy radiation he called an X-band because the equipment did not exist at the time to measure it. He designed a device which could record the effect on x-ray film. Other physicists replicating the experiments showed the same results but could not explain their observations. The idea that the movement of water underground could create a radiant energy did not fit the mold which physics had been pushed into in the 1930's.

Flanagan continued his research in vortices and developed a device capable of creating the "perfect vortex." He called the device the "vortex tangenital amplifier." Using this device he was able to lower the surface tension of water to an all time low of 26 dynes per centimeter, which is the same as ethyl alcohol. When water tension was lowered to the extreme was that it would revert to its normal surface tension rather than remain stable. It was found that at 38 dynes the surface tension could be maintained and last for years.

The basis of Flanagan's understanding dealt with the unique characteristics of the tiniest colloids. Large colloidal materials would lose their charge whereas the smallest particles would retain their charge, which made them optimally long lasting. The ability to retain the electrical charge is known as Zeta-potential.

Thomas Riddick, a colloidal chemist, says that Zeta-potential is what is responsible for the billions of circulating cells in the body maintaining their discreteness. He found that blood cells are kept in circulation by this Zeta-potential or negative electric charge. The entire living organism is made up of colloids which flow according to electrical attractions. Blood cells are coated with albumen a substance that allows them to maintain their charge and separateness from other blood cells. Unhealthy foods or high toxic levels in the blood, poor oxygen intake and other factors cause the blood to clump together, losing discrete form. This impairs the transfer of energy and the flow of nutrients through the system. Conversely, if you eat and drink highly charged colloids from fresh vegetables and fruit, or from the right forms of water, increased negative electric charges will be found on blood cells. This increases human health and energy.

The water Flanagan invented duplicated the key properties of Hunza water. He found that by adding only one teaspoon of the concentrated 38 dynes per centimeter water to a gallon of distilled water the surface tension would be between 55-65 dynes. This water when taken into the living organism changes the state of the cells within a few minutes. The cells of blood when observed under the microscope change from being clumped together to being separate and discrete.

The idea that this water's altered structure might have other beneficial uses was also explored. In one instance this newly engineered water was used in cement where the strength of the solidified concrete was increased from 8,400 pounds per square inch to 12,300 pounds per square inch. In another test on cement the air content of partially liquid cement was measured. It was found that the air content, which makes cement weaker, was only 30 percent verses 70 percent with ordinary water. In addition, the treated cement required less water and demonstrated greater flow and plasticity.

Flanagan found that reversing a vortical flow's direction caused increased potentializing of the water. This was the same mysterious energy found by earlier researchers and yet unexplained. What happens when the fluid is turning is that an amount of energy is present in the whirling flow of the water. When the flow is abruptly reversed the energy must go somewhere and, in this case, it has to be absorbed into the hydrogen bonds of the water. This increases the Zeta-potential, making the water more ingestible by living things. The change in direction causes the vortex to collapse by imploding or falling into itself. In so doing, what appears to be total chaos is, in reality, the formation of many vortices of water and exchanges of energy.

Flanagan worked to develop the highest energy potentials of the water he created with his newly discovered 33 step process. He knew that the higher the Zeta-potential achieved, the better in terms of removing toxins from the body and carrying nutrients throughout the living organism. The Microclusters® he created energize everything they come in contact with. When the University of Minnesota studied his invention they found that the size of the colloids was as small as five nanometers (five billionth of a meter). They are so small that 240,000 of them can be placed side by side on the head of a pin while at the same time they have an incredible surface area of 240,000 square feet per ounce.

Another way to illustrate this is to take a cube measuring one inch on each side. The total surface area is six square inches. The electrical charge is held on the surface of the substance.Therefore, the greater the surface area the greater the electrical charge. If we slice the cube into the thinnest possible slices we get an increase in surface area. For instance, if you just sliced the cube into one hundred slices you would have a surface area, front and back, of 200 square inches. Think of this illustration in terms of Microclusters® five billionth of a meter in size and the surface area they can cover.

When various nutrients are combined with Microclusters® they are enclosed in a geodesic sphere structure composed of a form of silica. These structures then carry the nutrients to the parts of the body where the cells can use them. These tiny nutrient and mineral combinations have unusual energy and catalytic abilities making them much more effective when they reach the cells.

Living Water

Another early researcher into the anomalies of water, Viktor Schauberger, concluded that life was based on implosions and death was based on explosions. He believed from his observations in nature and experiment-ation that this was the case. In his laboratory he built an egg shaped "vortex reaction chamber" which he also referred to as an "implosion chamber." These chambers caused the energy releases to flow to the center rather than toward the outer edges like an explosion. He believed that to optimize life things should flow with nature rather than act against natural flows.[33]

Viktor Schauberger observed that energy entering matter like water and air did so with inwardly spiraling energy. He observed that these inward spirals were the building forces of nature, imploding towards the center, the energy flows in life giving funnels of power. The energy of decaying forces on the other hand were always outflowing explosive energies. Based on these observa-tions in nature he believed this principle should be applied to technology.

Schauberger believed that the prevailing techno-

33 Secrets of the Soil, Vortex of Life, by Peter Tompkins & Christopher Bird, 1989, Pges 99 -115.

logy was using the wrong form of motion. These forces always scattered energy whereas nature uses a different kind of energy in creating order and growth by focusing inward. He warned that the system that men had adapted of burning fossil fuels and splitting atoms filled the world with heat-generating motion which flowed in the wrong direction. He believed that modern technology should use the principles of implosion, or inward flowing motion, in its future developments.

The Energy Exchange

The Microcluster® colloids produced by the Flanagans exhibit a property which is known as hydrophobic (hydra = water & phobic is a dislike of) hydration. Hydrophobic referrers to particles which have little or no affinity towards water. It was once thought that these kinds of particles would be suspended in an "iceberg quasi-crystalline" structure. What is now known is that these particles actually become suspended within cage-like structures formed by the water molecules. This increases the structured order of the water where the molecules then pack more closely together decreasing in volume and decreasing the surface tension of the water.

Entropy is a measure of the amount of unavailable energy which is also reflected as the amount of disorder or chaos in a system. The lower the entropy, the more energy is available and the more organized the system. Energy of entropy is directly related to the organization of structure. A system with low entropy is more organized than a system with high entropy. A system which displays maximum entropy is a system in chaos showing only random motion. By use of Micro-clusters® the organizational structure of the water is increased and entropy deceased, creating higher levels of "free energy" – energy available for other work.

When Microclusters® are added to the water the idea of hydrophobic hydration discussed earlier comes into play. What happens is that the water-disliking particles become trapped within a geodesic structure formed by the water molecules. As a result, the organization of the structure of the water changes and becomes increasingly more uniform. This can be thought of as a liquid crystalline structure. This causes the water molecules to pack more tightly resulting in a reduction of random movement, water volume and surface tension of the water.[34]

These structures, formed around the minute particles, do not bind to the particles themselves. The particles are trapped in suspension within their cages. These particles are then free to vibrate and rotate in suspension. The vibrational and rotational energies create patterns of energy throughout the newly structured water which form patterns that are similar to holograms.[35]

These observations might be applied to explaining homeopathy. Homeopathic treatments are used throughout Europe and Asia and have been for years. These remedies are based on the idea that water can act as a carrier of the "memory" of various elements and compounds which can then create reactions in the body causing healing. Homeopathy comes under attack from time to time because mainstream science, until recently, has had difficulty explaining why this system of healing works. In other words, what is observed does not line up with the current view of the science. The science has advanced and now is more clear in describing why some of these effects may occur.

In the process of preparing homeopathic remedies, hydrophobic hydration "cages" are formed around the remedy particles. These particles are then free to vibrate to their own unique frequency in these cages thereby producing energy waves which most likely produce holographic information patterns in the water structure. These information patterns may be picked up by the cells which then alter cellular processes. The use of

34 "Flanagan Microcluster® Colloids and Negative Entropy" by Patrick and Gael Crystal Flanagan, 1994.
35 Ibid.

Microcluster® colloids in the production of homeopathic remedies makes this process easier and more efficient. A few European homeopathic manufacturers are now using Flanagan Microcluster® colloids as carriers in their medications. The use of this technology increases the potency of the remedies.

Nutritional Formulas

All nutrients must be wetted before they can be used by the body. Nutrients can be divided into two general categories - those which are water soluble and those which are lipid or "oil" soluble. Lipid soluble nutrients are known as lipophilic or "oil loving" and water soluble nutrients are known as hydrophilic or "water loving."

All substances have a property referred to as Critical Surface Tension (CST). Critical Surface Tension is used to describe the level above which a substance can not be wetted. Water soluble nutrients have a higher CST than oil soluble substances.

Critical Surface Tension is based on the number of electrical charges on the surface of a substance. Water wets a substance by means of an electrical charge called hydrogen bonding. The hydrogen atoms in the water molecules are positively charged. In order to wet the surface of a substance the surface has to have free negative electrical charges on the surface. The greater the number of charges the more readily wetted. Oil has no electrical charge and as a result can not be wetted by water. Quartz crystal (silica) is highly charged and can be easily wetted by water.

Water soluble organic nutrients are only soluble in water which has a surface tension below the surface tension of the substance. If the water is ordinary tap water with high surface tension the nutrients will not be absorbed into the solution. If it is not absorbed into solution, the nutrients will not be efficiently transferred to the cells in the body. With Microclusters® the surface tension of the water is so significantly reduced that nutrients can be moved into the cells with great efficiency. The interaction resulting from the use of Microclusters® is that the nutrients become wetted to the point where they can be easily absorbed into the body and used.

Oil soluble nutrients can not be wetted by water. It is important to remember that Microclusters® are hydrophilic ("water loving) and lipophilic ("oil loving"). Oil particles can be trapped within a Microcluster® colloid. When oil particles are encapsulated in this way a tiny ball is created which is bound to water on the outside surfaces and to the oil on the inside surfaces.

These oil containing "cages" are very similar to what the body naturally produces when it digests oils. The body produces what are called chylomicrons which can be visualized as tiny spheres of oil which are coated with a covering of bile or other biological substances. Like the body's chylomicrons, Microclusters® have a negative surface charge or Zeta potential. It is the negative electrical charge which allows either a chylomicron or a Microcluster® sphere to be absorbed into the body. The absorption occurs through the lymphatic system from the intestines. These particles by-pass the liver on their first entrance into the body.[36]

The amount of Microcluster® powder used in formulating the solution is dependent on the surface area to be covered and the CST of the original nutrient. Remember that the particle size has a relationship to surface area: the amount needed to cover the surface is relatively small. The smaller the size, the higher the surface area of a similar mass of the nutrient. The key is making sure that enough of the Microcluster solution is present to ensure complete wetting so that the nutrient can

[36] Dr. E. M. Carlisle of the University of California, reported in "Trace Elements in Animal and Human Nutrition" , that silica is "absorbed through the intact intestinal mucosa, pass through the lymphatic and circulatory systems, and reach other tissues supplied by arterial blood via the alveolar region of the lung."

be absorbed by the body.

Some nutrients can be destroyed by the liver. The use of Microclusters® for encapsulating these nutrients in the geodesic cages described earlier allow for these to by-pass the liver and be absorbed by the lymphatic system. Particles as large as five microns in diameter can be absorbed whole into the lymphatic system if they can get by the liver. What this means is that very large nutrients with high molecular weights can be easily distributed into the lymphatic pathway by-passing the destruction by the liver.[37]

According to Dr. Patrick Flanagan, "In the digestive system, nutrient absorption depends on the wetting of nutrients by water. The wetting process depends on surface tension: The lower the surface tension of the digestive fluids, the more effective will be the nutrient absorption. There are three sites of absorption in the digestive system. Alcohol is the only nutrient absorbed by the stomach. Carbohydrates, amino acids and other nutrients that are water soluble are absorbed through the 'hepatic' pathway from the small intestine. The portal vein carries these nutrients to the liver where they are further processed before being used by the body."[38] Microclusters® lower the surface tension in water which allows for the increase in efficiency in nutrient transfers into the body.

Looking at the Microcluster®

Dr. Alex Carrel won the Nobel Prize in medicine for demonstrating that living cells can be kept alive indefinitely. Dr. Carrel said, "The cell is immortal. It is merely the fluid in which it floats that degenerates. Renew this fluid at intervals, give the cells what they require for nutrition, and as far as we know, the pulsation of life may go on forever."

37 <u>Earthstar</u>, Vol. XIV No. 88, "Drs. Gael Crystal and Patrick Flanagan, Putting the 'Physics' Back in Metaphysics" October/November 1992.
38 Ibid.

The fluid that this researcher was referring to is cellular water. Cellular water has unique form because it is structured out of liquid crystals as opposed to ordinary water which lacks liquid crystal form. Many attempts to duplicate Dr. Carrel's work have met with failure because other researchers were unable to duplicate his secret solution used in vitalizing the cells. The secret of long cell life is in the energy mediator which is found in the fluids of all living things. The mediator may have been discovered by Dr. Gaston Naessens of Canada. He called the cellular energy transformer a "somatid" which means "tiny body."

The discovery made by Dr. Naessens could not have been made without the invention of a new and powerful microscope. Dr. Naessens microscope allowed him to see objects never visible to the human eye and which could not be seen using ordinary microscopes or electron microscopes.

In his early research (1940's) as a microbiologist, he observed something in the blood which could barely be seen under the best microscopes of that time. He knew that the ability to see an object under a microscope was dependent on the ability to illuminate the object. He discovered a way to create a much more powerful microscope. He was successful in inventing the Naessens Microscope, now available to researchers. This is one of the tools which Dr. Patrick and Gael Crystal Flanagan have used in their research into water and other areas.

Patrick and Gael Flanagan have made good use of this invention, using it to observe these ultra-small energy mediators – somatids. These somatids look like tiny flickering points of pure light which appear to dance around live human blood cells. These super small points of light are in the body fluids of all living things from plants to animals. In fresh vegetables these somatids are found in abundance. As fresh food ages the number of somatids deceases, as does the vitality of the food.

What Dr. Gael Crystal Flanagan noted was that, "In foods, we have found that live, organic raw fruits and vegetables as well as their juices quickly affect the blood in a positive way. The discreteness and mobility of blood cells and somatids are rapidly enhanced. The microscope has enabled us to rapidly see the difference between organic vital food and devitalized and processed foods."[39] The Flanagans observed that poisons and pollutants destroy the energy or Zeta-potential of foods.

The research conducted by the Flanagans correlates what was observed in plants with humans. The Flanagans found profound changes in blood samples after the use of Microclusters®. They found that the concentration of somatids markedly increases with the ingestation of water treated with Microclusters®. Moreover, when feeling tired and sluggish a direct correlation between the density or concentration of somatids in the blood was observed. They found somatids in Hunza water, Crystal Energy® and fruits and vegetables. By observing somatids concentrations in their blood after eating, sleeping, exercising and other activities the Flanagan's have designed a lifestyle with maximum energy levels.

They also found that certain specific nutrients had a profound effect on human blood. Vitamin B12, for instance, has unique electrical properties which cause them to function as energy transducers, changing the energy from one form to another. They found that the best type of B12 was co-enzyme B12 which is the form naturally stored in the human body. When this form is taken it bypasses the body's five-part natural B12 manufacturing process. Dr. Gael Flanagan explains that, "The reason vitamin B12 is energizing to the body is that all tetrapyrrole or porphyrin ring type structures act as energy transformers for the living system. The algae Spirulina contains an enormous quantity of these

39 Earthstar, Vol. XIV No. 88, "Drs. Gael Crystal and Patrick Flanagan, Putting the 'Physics' Back in Metaphysics" October/November 1992.

pigments including co-enzyme B12."[40]

The Flanagans found that Adenosine Tri-phosphate (ATP), as the energy giving molecule, has a powerful effect on blood when it is delivered to the fluid outside of cells. Normally, ATP is manufactured and used inside of cells rather than on the outside. Very little ATP appears on the outside of the cells in the lymphatic fluids which are found there. Research has shown that this energetic substance has a powerful effect on the outside of the cells, acting like a powerful neurotrans-mitter. In this case it exerts a powerful influence on extra (outside) cellular receptors. Fresh natural foods contain an abundance of ATP.

The Flanagans, through this microscopic research into blood, were able to observe the effects of foods most American ingest regularly. These processed and fat laden foods thicken and devitalize the blood. They also observed that many products contain aluminum such as deodorants and antacids. Aluminum is a small atom which has a triple positive valence and wreaks havoc with the negatively charged blood. According to the Flana-gans, aluminum entering the body through aluminum cans, cookware and as additives in various products should be avoided.

Imbalances between potassium and sodium or calcium and magnesium could have profound effects on blood. Most processed foods are devitalized partially because they reverse the concentration of these important nutrients. Natural foods contain more of the right proportions of the correct nutrients which food processing reverses. In the case of sodium/potassium balances natural foods contain as much as five times the potassium as sodium. In the case of magnesium/calcium balances, natural foods contain twice the magnesium as processed foods. The proper proportion of these nutrients is critical to blood balance and good health.

40 Earthstar, Vol. XIV No. 88, "Drs. Gael Crystal and Patrick Flanagan, Putting the 'Physics' Back in Metaphysics" October/November 1992.

Excess magnesium moves calcium from the softer tissues in the body into the bones where it is needed. When calcium is in excess, hormones are released which move calcium away from the bones into the softer tissue where the excess calcium ions destroy cells.

The Flanagans research has shown the importance of eating the right foods in the right form. Also, their research reinforces the role of water as a carrier for energy and nutrients transfer into the body and a remover of toxins. By adding Microclusters® colloids, increased efficiency in the nutrient transfer process occurs. If food and vitamins are spread out over the day and combined with the right water, the body can increase the efficiency of those transfers even more.

The circulation of blood is also significantly enhanced by exercises such as T'ai Chi Chuan, walking and yoga. Breathing exercises are also powerful body vitality enhancers. Health can be significantly enhanced with the right combination of diet and water. This is one of the keys to maintaining health and vitality as we age.

Their life's research has led the Flanagans down a number of unusual paths. Through their diverse work they have studied the energy which flows through the acupuncture points as well as other subtle energies in the body. They have constructed instruments which can measure these very fine bioenergies. They have shown that the energy around the human body can be altered by diet, exercise, attitude, water intake and a number of other factors. The changes in the overall energy state of the body can be dramatic.

Chapter 9

Pyramids and Geometric Energy

I have always had an intellectual curiosity about geometry and forms. The formulas and mathematics in geometry were interesting and it seemed that there must be more connected to it. In the mid 1970's my good friend John Chandler gave me a copy of a paper by Patrick Flanagan called The Pyramid and Its Relationship to Biocosmic Energy and later I ran across a book by Flanagan called *Pyramid Power*. These were both interesting because they were written to interpret and explain the energy of certain geometric shapes.

Flanagan was one of the earlier researchers on pyramids and the first real researcher on energies which emanate from these unique three dimensional object. The work undertaken by him in his research led to a number of books including that first book, *Pyramid Power*. This hard cover book was written in a week and sold over one and a half million copies. Looking back to 1973, the publication of the book was, for many people, one of the triggering events which led to their exploration of new ideas regarding subtle energies. An early pioneer, Flanagan is one of the elders of the new shift in science we are witnessing.

In 1978, I was a guest speaker at the International Biorhythm Association's meeting in Atlanta, Georgia, where I met Dr. Reijo Makela. We explored the idea that there was a geometrics in sound wave relationships which might explain why certain sound waves had been reported to have beneficial effects on people and plants. Since that time much more research has been done in this area. The idea that energy exchanges could be enhanced by the shape of an object should not be so difficult to grasp. All objects receive and transfer energy in some way, at some level. The shape of an object, and not just the material it is constructed of, can also facilitate more efficient transfers of energy. Transferred energy takes a variety of forms including electrical energy, heat, light and sound. The way energy is handled in relationship to shape should not really be so startling.

In 1978, Reijo Makela published a book called _Life and Death = Wave Propagation_. The book was the outgrowth of his work and contained a reference to some of our conversations while in Atlanta. In Makela's words:

_"Calculations show that if any kind of cone or pyramid is placed at the center pole between two poles in an electromagnet it will increase the magnetic flux lines both in volume and flux density. Thus a very high flux density will be created at the apex of the cone or pyramid. The addition of the cone will increase the surface area of high flux of the magnet. The cone or pyramid will reduce the electricity consumption of the electromagnet. There are no mysterious "pyramid powers" - only forces in field and rotational form which can be calculated by using quantum mechanical laws and accounting for the rotational power, which is not an electromagnetic force as such, but it always accompanies electromagnetic phenomena."_41

"It is known that pyramids do indeed cause various things to happen, including measurable effects on the human brain. The effects can be measured as changes in the energy's electromagnetic behavior. If we accept the fact that pyramids are built on normal electrically charged ground and are receiving radiation (from the sun's rays) in polarized and unpolarized form . The rays include

41 Life and Death = Wave Propagation, by Dr. Reijo Makela, Brisbane, Australia, ISBN 0-9595511-0-7, 1978, pges 55-57.

*frequencies far outside the visible spectrum, these rays penetrate the crystallographic material of the pyramid."*42

*"The angles of the pyramid are such that they form an axis in which an electromagnetic wave is propagated without double refraction. Thus the waves are separated from each other and each frequency or rotational force "works independently" - until it meets another wave which has exactly the same frequency and thus the same rotational force. When these two waves (or a large number of similar waves) meet, the force formed is that of resonance: not the sum of waves, but the sum of the waves squared (multiplied against itself). That means that at the top of the cone or pyramid, the rotatory force is very high, this can be also measured as marked increases in the magnetic fields."*43

The Search for Biocosmic Energy

Patrick Flanagan attacked his interest in this subject by reading everything he could find about pyramids. He also traveled to Egypt on over 30 separate occasions in pursuing his research. The whole issue of subtle or unknown energies was of great interest to him.

In the late 1960's and early 1970's Flanagan had been researching what he called Biocosmic Energy. This was Flanagan's word for what he believed was the energy coming from the pyramid. The concept of life energy relating to the universe was encompassed in the root of the idea of biocosmic energies. This was not some mystical form of energy but, rather, energy which was understood millennia ago and only rediscovered in modern times.

As a scientist, Flanagan felt challenged to study, quantify and then use his knowledge of this force creatively. The idea that this force, or energy, might be used to enhance mankind intrigued him. The energy had

42 Life and Death = Wave Propagation, by Dr. Reijo Makela, Brisbane, Australia, ISBN 0-9595511-0-7, 1978, pges 55-57.
43 Ibid.

been known both in esoteric and scientific literature but without much in the way of scientific explanation.

The energy had been referred to by a number of names over the years, including Life Energy, Bioplasmic Energy, Odic Force, Prana, Mana, Magnale Magnum, N-Rays, Etheric Force, Psychotronic Energy, Kundalini, Chi, and many other names. Although there have been thousands of books on the subject of this energy, most were shrouded in religious and occult mysticism rather than a framework of science. Because the idea of this energy was surrounded by religious mysticism main-stream scientists avoided research into the area. Patrick, always the maverick, dove into this research, consuming over 300 rare books and manuscripts on the subject. He concluded that all of the descriptions, regardless of the word used to describe the energy, contained the same basic matrix of ideas. The correlations were unmistak-able, leaving him with a clear understanding that they were all describing the same thing.[44]

Flanagan's curiosity was piqued when he was 14 years old and in the midst of developing film in his dark room. As mentioned elsewhere in this book, while he was at work with the film he was wearing his Neurophone®, which caused his skin to be effected by the fields created by the device. As he developed his film he noticed images of his fingers on the film. The images had what appeared to be energy fields around his fingers. The radio frequency energy from his device was somehow stimulating a secondary energy emission of visible light which was being picked up by the photographic film. Years later Flanagan would read about Russian researcher Semyon Davidovich Kirlian who in 1939 observed a similar effect which led to 14 patents in the area of Kirlian Photography – a system for photographing human energy fields.[45]

---

44 "The Pyramid and Its Relationship to Biocosmic Energy", a paper prepared by Patrick Flanagan, 1972.
45 Psychic Discoveries Behind the Iron Curtain, by Sheila Ostrander and Lynn Schroeder, 1970, pages 200-210.

The Russian theory for Kirlian photography was that when a living organism or an object was charged with high frequency, high voltage electricity, the electrical corona will flow with the natural lines of force leaving the object or organism. These lines of force are said to be sub-atomic particles, a "cold plasma" surrounding all living organisms and around all electric and magnetic fields.

The energy observations by the young scientist Flanagan caused him to try and find a better explanation for the effect and a way to measure the energy. The tool to measure these biological energy flows had to be extremely sensitive. After a number of trials a device was designed. This device added a good deal to the research in that it provided a way to measure effects in terms of magnitude.

He found that the energy from the pyramids had unique properties, that when raw meat was placed on a plate constructed out of pyramids and allowed to sit at room temperature it would not rot. Instead, the meat would dry out and mummify rather than decay. He also found that the taste of food would improve by just setting it, for a time, on these pyramid biocosmic energy plates.46

In Flanagan's research, he found that the shape of the pyramid at Giza in Egypt was capable of producing this subtle but powerful form of energy. What Flanagan saw in all of this in 1972 was a new kind of science, a new field, he called "Magnetic Form Resonance"47. It is interesting to note that now in 1996, we have magnetic imaging resonance which produces some of the finest images of the human body yet.

What Flanagan believed is that these energies could be "tuned" by using devices like pyramids. By tuning the

46 "The Pyramid and Its Relationship to Biocosmic Energy", a paper prepared by Patrick Flanagan, 1972.
47 Ibid.

History

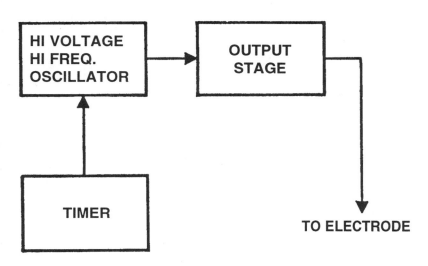

FIGURE IV

Kirlian photography set-up

Pyramid Power

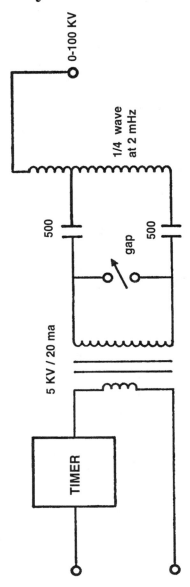

FIGURE XVII

High frequency high voltage oscillator for Kirlian photography.

energy, beneficial results might be possible such as those observed with the plates he had constructed out of pyramids. He believed that what was being observed was the actual force which binds the universe together. These subtle energy fields had been missed by others as the true nature of the energy went beyond the photographable field of blue and pink energy. It was being emitted from, and conducted by, organic electrical insulators. It behaved like heat, magnetism and light but was, in and of itself, none of these. It was biocosmic energy - a new energy form. The study of this energy was, in many respects, what Flanagan's work has always been about. It is about the transfer of energy from one form into another using the medium of science rather than the cage of mysticism.

The energy readings from the device Flanagan constructed, and from Kirlian photography, show that emotions and other physical and mental states change the energy condition of the bioplasmic energy. These energies were measured by Flanagan using very sensitive magnetometers and electrostatic field meters. He also found that when a pyramid was placed in a metal box which shielded it from the Earth's naturally occurring magnetic field, the energy effects changed. The pyramid, when shielded, no longer had the ability to preserve meat and energize foods. The orientation of the pyramid outside of a shielded environment was also important. In order to magnify or focus this energy the most efficiently it had to be oriented with the magnetic north pole.

Flanagan discovered that the pyramid's properties would be altered if the magnetic fields of the Earth were altered in the area where it was being used. It could be interfered with by electrical or plumbing systems as well as by the operation of some electrical appliances.

Energy History

The ideas of subtle energies have gone by many names. The basic premise seems the same - that all life flows from energy, that all matter is an outgrowth of energy. The ancient alchemist fully engaged in trying to create changes in elements altering their form and energy matrix. But what else were these old wizards all about? The thrust of their work was trying to discover the essence of life and matter. Their ideas were combinations of religious, philosophic and scientific thinking joined to form obscure investigations. Man's interest in energy is not new. Much has been written and even more perhaps lost in the language translations and over time. In modern history we recognize the Einstein formula as the expression of the idea of energy being changed into matter:

$$E = Mc^2$$

Energy ideas are as old as man. The oldest known word for energy is an ancient Egyptian word Ga-llama which describes the very foundation of existence. It means that with every indrawn breath you take on new life. Prana is "absolute energy" in Sanskrit and still retains this meaning in Hindu Yoga. It is the basic life energy. The yogis believe that the air we breath is charged with prana and when breath is taken into the lungs energy accompanies the breath. They believe that proper breathing increases energy in the body. This has been supported by modern science as well and although the words describing the observations are different, the measured effects are similar.

The ancients believed that energy traveled defined paths within the human body and through seven primary energy centers called "chakras." It is believed that the amount of prana taken into the body would have an effect on the outer energy field of the body. They also believed that a reservoir of energy existed at the base of the spine. They called this energy Kundalini and symbolized it with a serpent coiled three and a half times. It is believed that by taking in prana, and focusing energy, the Kundalini energy would rise through the centers and manifest in the person as a source for vision and creative energy.

The Tibetans in monasteries of northern India call

the life force Tumor. The monks of these regions are able to withstand subfreezing temperatures completely naked at over 18,000 foot elevations. The word Tumor means heat, warmth and fire but when the word is used it is not referring to ordinary fire or warmth. These monks are masters of this energy in their bodies and have been known to radiate enough heat to melt snow up to twenty feet away.

Chi is a name given to energy by the ancient Chinese. It is the vital energy which flows through all living things. The Chinese practice of acupuncture is based on the principles of this energy. The energy meridians, or paths, through which this energy flows have been well documented. In fact the points which are the focal points for the energy actually show a difference in their electrical properties compared to the surrounding skin. In the 1960's the Soviets had developed a detector, the "tobiscope" which was used for measuring these properties and could be used for locating the acupuncture points.

In the 1930's, Dr. Alexander Gurvich, a Russian scientist, discovered that all living cells produced an invisible radiation which he called "mitogenic radiation." Dr. Gurvich succeeded in photographing these rays, which he published in a paper called "I Rug Della vita fotografati." In human subjects the doctor discovered that blood, the eye and nerves all radiated mitogenic rays.

Based on this research the Soviets concluded that all life forms radiated this energy and that the state of the energy could be manipulated. The manipulation of these fields could result in good or adverse health effects. Moreover, they confirmed what the Hindus had said for years - that prana was in the air and could be converted into energy. The Soviets found that oxygen from the air contained energy which would transform into bioplasmic energy. They also found that deep breathing exercises tended to revitalize the body and reorient energy patterns in the body. Their experiments also confirmed the effects of color, negative air ions and other external forces on this energy body.

The various researchers in the areas of energy fields around the body have found that it can be reflected, refracted, polarized and combined with other forms of energy. It could create effects similar to electricity, magnetism, heat, and light, but was separate and distinct from all of these. It was also found that this energy could somehow be conducted, or transferred, through known conductive materials as well as through what were otherwise thought to be insulators.

Measuring The Fields

A number of devices exist for measuring the different energy fields around the body in addition to charting their flows. These new technologies only serve to demonstrate what the Chinese knew thousands of years ago. We can now quantify these energy flows and fields taking them out of the realm of "mystery and religion" and placing them into the area of scientific investigation.

Besides the differences in electrical properties of the skin there is also a static voltage field around all living things. This field can be affected by the mind. Using a special kind of field meter, differences in a person's energy state can be mapped and even the field changes caused by the beating of the heart can be picked up over three feet away.

There also exists a magnetic field around the body. The equipment necessary to measure this field can be very expensive and difficult to obtain. However, Dr. Flanagan suggests another way of measuring the changes in the magnetic field around a person: "the person to be measured is to lie down on his back on the floor. An ordinary magnetic compass is suspended over the solar plexus region on the body a few inches above. If the subject is then given pain, as in a severe pinch, the compass needle will deflect considerably."[48]

The energy surrounding the body has a complex field structure that can be impacted by internal and external factors. We are bathed in a sea of energy most of which we pass through without notice. We are immersed in the magnetic fields of the Earth and those between the Earth and the ionosphere.

It happens that the Earth pulsates at .1 to 100 cycles per second with major components in the 8 to 16 cycles per second range. This is the same range as predominant brain frequencies in humans. The human brain will entrain to these frequencies. In other words our brains will oscillate with the natural predominate rhythms of the Earth.

It has been shown that the magnetic fields of the Earth have a strong effect on life. Plants denied access to these natural magnetic fields do not grow properly. These natural fields bend and warp around us and our dwellings. Modern homes and offices tend to shield or distort these natural energy fields thereby removing us from their positive influences. Inadequate exposure to these fields can result in fatigue, irritability and apathy.[49]

Ark of the Covenant

Understanding these properties of magnetic fields, Flanagan has even developed a theory about the Ark of the Covenant. The Ark of the Covenant was designed to protect the written promise of God. It was described in Exodus 25:10-21 as being a large box made of wood and gold. If this box were constructed today it would have some very unusual characteristics according to Flanagan. The box would in fact be a very large capacitor with the capability of being charged by the Earth's natural electrostatic field. He suggests that its design would allow

48 Pyramid Power, by G. Pat Flanagan, 1973. Library of Congress Number 73-86022.
49 Electromagnetic Fields and Life, by Dr. A.S. Pressman, Plenum Press, N.Y., 1970.

it to build energy to between 600 and 1000 volts and could store enough power so as to kill anyone who touched it. It is interesting to note that the coffer in the King's Chamber of the Great Pyramid is the same proportion as the Ark of the Covenant.

Pyramid Research

Flanagan looked at the earlier research conducted by others on the Great Pyramid. He duplicated the work of Bevies and Dryable, who had recognized the strange energy properties of the pyramid in preserving meat. His research, however, had the advantage of new and highly sensitive measuring devices. Using these, Flanagan was able to determine that the entire interior and the apex of the pyramid had these mystery energies. The greatest concentration was in what was called the King's Chamber which is located in the center of the pyramid about one third of the way up.

Flanagan researched other shapes of various proportions and found that none of these had the special properties of a pyramid such as the one at Giza.

The Math

The math is not very complex when considered carefully. The mathematics illustrated in the proportion of the pyramid has a direct correlation to the mathematics of living things. The proportions reflected in the body of men, plants and animals have a mathematical equivalent expressed in the form and structure of the great pyramid – Phi. This shape could press energy into a specific routed path which focuses the energy. A pyramid could be thought of as a giant machine with no moving parts.

The Great Pyramid is a precise mathematical structure based upon the mathematical ratio of Phi and Pi. Foundationally, the pyramid can be reduced to just the mathematics of Phi because Pi can be mathematically stated in terms of Phi. What is Phi? This is again where science, religion and mysticism merge.

Phi is a mystical number used in architecture and painting proportions by the old masters.50 It was understood by Renaissance painters and architects. These artists thought that it was the most pleasing proportion to the human eye. They called this ratio the sacred cut. The ratio is 1.618 and is called Phi. The human anatomy is based on this ratio. In addition, a five pointed star's diagonals divide each other by this ratio.

The mathematics is a summation series which can be described as a series of numbers who's sequence is determined by adding the last two numbers together to get the next number. In the case of Phi it is 1, 2, 3, 5, 8, 13, 21, 34, 55, 89, 144, 233,377...etc. The mathematical constant is a ratio which can be calculated by dividing any number by its predecessor. The higher the numbers used, the more precise the number of the ratio as it approaches Phi.

The dimensions of the Great Pyramid are of some interest. The size is immense and its precision construction can not be duplicated today. The measurement used in its construction, the pyramid inch, was equal to one Thea part of the Earth's diameter at the poles. From this unit of measure the Great Pyramid conveys the length of a year on Earth as 365.24 days and the length of our equinox at 25,827 years. The temperature inside the King's chamber is a constant 68 degrees which is said to be the ideal temperature for health and long life. It is also equal to exactly 1/10th the temperature it takes to boil water at sea level.

The Pyramid is aligned on its axis so that if you extend a line around the Earth in both directions the land mass of the planet will be equally divided. The alignment is incredible. The advanced mathematics needed to construct this again demonstrates our lack of understanding with respect to the intellectual state of our

---

50 Sacred Geometry, by Robert Lawlor 1982, ISBN 0-500-81030-3.

ancestors.

Testing the Energy

For Patrick Flanagan, demonstrating the effect of the shape was important. It had been proven by a European scientist, Dryable, that a razor blade could be sharpened by leaving it in a pyramid. This test was duplicated by Flanagan with his blades delivering over two hundred shaves where otherwise they lasted only three or four shaves. Dryable believed that the crystal structure of the blade changed. However, Patrick theorized that it could be because of the well known principle that electromagnetic energy tends to discharge from the sharpest points on an object.

Flanagan used Kirlian photography, galvanic skin resistance (GSR) measurements of the acupuncture points, alpha wave detectors and subjective responses of test subjects.

In the Kirlian photography tests he was able to demonstrate that there was a measurable change in the energy surrounding living things. He would take a Kirlian photograph of a test subject's fingers for from one minute to a half an hour just prior to entering a pyramid structure. The results varied somewhat but the overall energy visible in the field surrounding the body increased in size, texture and strength.

The same tests were performed on plants with startling results. A leaf from a geranium plant was removed from the plant and left for a half an hour and then photographed. The photograph showed very little energy surrounding the plant - the leaf was dying. After a five minute treatment in a pyramid, the energy field around the plant had increased considerably.

Galvanic skin resistance (GSR) instruments were used to test plants when enclosed in a pyramid structure. Overall current resistance was lowered as soon as the

Pyramid Power

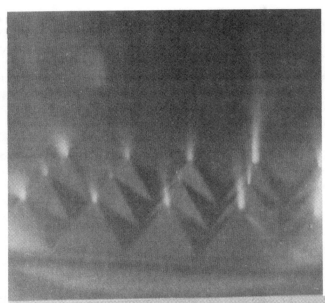

FIGURE XXIII
**Pyramid grid or matrix uses radiation of
energy from the points of the pyramid.**

plant was enclosed, except if the plant was in a rest state. The plants natural rest state was detectable on the meter of the GSR device. The plant indicated a response by meter movement when someone else entered the room, when the color of the lighting changed, or in reaction to the observer's heart rhythm, stress and even thoughts.

GSR measurements of human subjects were also explored. In all cases rapid changes in skin resistance occurred when subjects were in a pyramid for as little as five minutes time. The skin resistance between acupuncture points was in some cases lowered from 150,000 ohms to 2,500 ohms. It appeared that the structure balanced the Qi energy flow between the acupuncture meridians.

In plant growth experiments with alfalfa sprouts the results were powerful. Flanagan used three different approaches; 1. Water treatment prior to feeding the sprouts; 2. Direct treatment of the plant by housing it in a pyramid; and, 3. Treatment of the seeds in a pyramid. The results were best by direct treatment of the plant and treatment of the water. The least effective was treatment of the seeds, although this was somewhat effective as well. The plants grew two to three times faster and lasted twice as long after harvesting. Foods, fresh cut plants, cigarettes, bananas and other perishables were all affected positively by pyramid energies.

The Sensor®

Tibetan mystics have said for thousands of years that certain geometric designs have special power. They believe that these designs can have profound effects on our physical and psychic states. The Tibetans developed a type of Yoga they call Yantra. Yantra Yoga in the ancient language of Sanskrit means "geometric power design."

In addition to Flanagan's investigations into pyramid energy he also investigated the Yantra Effect. He found that the energy which emanates from certain designs had a striking similarity to the energy concentrated and flowing from pyramids.

As a result of his investigations he created a special energy design which he stamped out as a metal medallion. These machines produced powerful energy effects without moving parts or a power source outside of the energy fields which naturally surrounded the device. He called these devices Sensor® I, II, III and the Phi Ray Design®. These medallions act as "log-periodic Tuned Paramagnetic Amplifiers" for paramagnetic energy in the far infrared band. It is this energy band that Dr. Philip Callahan (University of Florida, Gainesville) has found plays a vital role in all living systems including people.

A one inch diameter medallion has the equivalent ability of concentrating energy as a six foot pyramid. The device can be worn with a significant increase in energy levels being created for the person wearing the object. The effects of these medallions have been proven with very sensitive instruments which are capable of sensing bioenergtic fields and emissions.

Dr. Callahan has an instrument which can measure subtle energy emissions. The tool is called a Fourier Transform Interferometer and can detect coherent (laser-like) energy in the far infrared band. This was the first machine ever designed to measure this energy and was originally manufactured in the early 1980's by Digi-Lab of Cambridge, Massachusetts.

In 1981 Dr. Callahan and Dr. Flanagan discovered that the Sensor® design acts like a powerful paramagnetic amplifier for the infrared waveband. This seventeen octave waveband was once known as the x-band because scientists did not have the detectors to differentiate the various wavelengths which comprise it. This band is the largest and least understood of all of the wavebands according to Flanagan.

Research carried out by the two scientists

confirmed that energy was released within this band when certain words were uttered or chanted by individuals. Moreover, when the Sensor® was held next to the Fourier Transform Interferometer the energy released and measured was dramatic. The Sensor® acted as a powerful paramagnetic amplifier causing thirty-three organic molecules to emit coherent laser-lines in the waveband from thirty-three micrometers to one millimeter in wavelength. This range of wavelengths is considered an important biological energy range.

Many of the emissions that the Sensor® can amplify are in the region of the infrared absorption bands found in water. Tests performed by the scientists using a Fisher Model 21 DuNuoys ring surface tensiometer (used to measure the surface tension of fluids) showed a dramatic increase in the free energy content of water. Ordinary water has a surface tension of 73 dynes per centimeter at room temperature. If surface tension can be reduced at the same temperature then the amount of free energy is increased.Tests performed by Flanagan showed that the surface tension of water can be reduced up to twenty dynes/cm in just a few moments time. This change indicates a very dramatic increase in available energy.

Tests were performed by Sheldon Deal, D.C., N.D., president of the International College of Applied Kinesiology in Tucson, Arizona. He was amazed at the effects of the Sensor® when it was placed on the body or very close to a person. He found that the effects were so strong that he could not diagnose his patients for weaknesses if they were wearing the device.The Sensor® had to be removed prior to Kinesiology testing.

The Merging Of Energy

Gael and Patrick Flanagan met under the most unusual circumstances. It was as if they were destined to meet and merge their life energy streams into a rushing river of change. Each of them brings to the relationship experience, talent and creativity which makes huge reserves of energy available in their effort to improve human conditions. Their work is moved forward with minimal stress as they press through each new effort with the smoothness of an indrawn breathe.

Gael had been living in the Bahamas in the early 1980's when she had a vivid dream which she could not shake from her consciousness. In the dream, she saw a man seated at a small table telling her about some important event which was about to take place in her life. She could not remember what the important event was, but it was the kind of dream that shakes you, that stays with you and seems to carry an energy of its own.

Two years later Gael was preparing to travel to the South Pacific when she ran across a brochure advertising a seminar in Scottsdale, Arizona. The seminar included a lecturer she was familiar with from his written work, Patrick Flanagan, "the father of pyramid power". Although she rarely attended seminars, she was prompted by Spirit to journey to Arizona for this particular event. As Gael prepared to go she recalled the dream of two years before.

Leading up to the July seminar both Patrick and Gael had experienced events which kept pointing toward some important event in their individual lives. While delivering his lecture Patrick required a volunteer and, out of a crowd of hundreds, Gael was selected. In the moment of their contact they were both struck by a recognition that each was somehow connected to the other. This recognition in the weeks that followed could not be designed, as repeated events of Spirit continued to move them towards each other, towards a new alchemy of change.

Their relationship continued to develop in the coming months and was crystallized in their marriage. They were married in the King's Chamber of the Great Pyramid in Giza, Egypt during the Pleiadian alignment of

1983, an event which occurs every 4,800 years.51

This was the beginning of a new direction, a force which created internal changes propelling external projections which continue to move them through the spiritual river of life.

Merged

The combination of open inquiry and scientific proofs are the hallmarks of the Flanagan's work together. They merge many of the ideas which have been expressed throughout time without clear explanation. The results are always startling for those on the outside looking in but, after careful consideration, are shown for what they are – myth dispelling realities which press into the millennium science. The future work of the Flanagans, as they build on their ideas, will provide opportunities to the rest of the world to see a ray of light, a hope in a place of dark clouds. They come from a Spirit center which flows unrestrained through the essence of who they are, into the reality of this world.

Patrick Flanagan's work with defining and describing pyramid and Sensor® energies and a geometric structures effects on energy continues to be an area of interest to him. The interest in energy extended into many other aspects of his research. So, from the esoteric to the scientific, the relationships of a new science were taking form. Flanagan has been one of the pioneers of a shift in scientific possibilities which require a new energetic look into the future.

---

51 <u>Destined to Love,</u> by Brad Streiger, 1996.

Chapter 10

God, Science and Change

From my initial meeting with Patrick and Gael Flanagan three years ago things have never been the same. The chase for new information and the recognition of the need to move forward has never been more clear. Where does it go from here? The answer is focused in consciousness. There is a great need for knowledge and technologies which support individual freedom and advancement. These are the things of the Spirit, the new science, the new alchemy and the change.

The time for change in the way we approach the decades ahead is **now**. In this very moment, as you read these words, rests the power for a new revolution in our individual paths. We control the elements of change within ourselves and it is individual action which frees the power of Spirit to interact with us. Nothing happens standing still. We are each part of an organic Internet requiring no human leader, no Board of Directors and no base of operation. We are able to link by our connection to each other through high spiritual values and belief systems which propel us into the action of creating human progress. This power of connection moves beyond all imposed limits, moves beyond all perceived realities and truly engages the complete energy source of which we are each a part, whether we see it or not.

At this juncture in the human experience many are feeling overwhelmed by the advancements being made in all fields of human endeavor. Some seek to slow the wave of change but can not grasp it. They can not hold what they do not understand. To stop the flow of energy is impossible. What **is** possible is to direct the energy flow into the next millennium. The energy is propelled by either good or bad intentions This is where the solution is found. Rightly motivated people can create the kind of changes which are needed now is not beyond our reach.

People throughout the world are seeking a new kind of leader whether it be in science, politics, religion or business. People are transferring their individual power to these new age leaders without consideration of the potent energy which resides in each of us individually. Perhaps the greatest lesson learned from my new friends, Drs. Patrick and Gael Crystal Flanagan, has been that – within each of us, resides a flow of power which can indeed move mountains. Most of us have a tendency to seek a source, a direction, from outside ourselves, from other human beings or from sources which seem to have the answers while missing the greatest connection and movement towards change – our own inner link to God.

Patrick Flanagan represents the best in science. His genius places him above the intellect of most people and yet he knows that the root of all knowledge resides in Spirit rather than in flesh. He recognizes the potency of this inner energy which presses outwardly into the reality which we all share in shaping. To what ends are we each adding to the shaping of this reality?

What I know from my experience with the Flanagans, and others like them, is that we are here to assist one another in an effort to improve the human condition. At first, perhaps this idea seems beyond our individual grasp but, then, it strikes us – we can **try** to make a difference. It is in the **trying** that the power towards change, towards the new alchemy, resides. It is not necessary to always win each pursuit, however, it is critical to make the effort. In the effort resources are always provided, lessons learned and progress made.

Rightly motivated seekers will eventually find the answers and discover how their energy is best suited for the change. Seeking within, and projecting without, is the culmination of this creativity.

The Flanagans motivated me as a writer with their encouragement. They pointed out my own ability to tell a story and deliver information. They softly encouraged the work, first on HAARP[52] and then in other areas. They gently awakened me to a greater potential. This was done not by taking power but by giving power. Leadership does not take control of people, it releases them to their own inner spirit.

My wife Shelah and I spent one of the final weeks of our research for this book in Sedona, Arizona, the home of the Flanagans. The week was primarily set aside to spend time with our friends and review the draft of this book. The trip to the southwest was again a catalyst for change. Joining us there were two other seekers and friends who have committed themselves to assisting people in awakening to their own potentials and their individual connections to that which is universal – the very essence of creativity and power, the energy which is God.

For the six of us gathering in Sedona it was a time which marked the beginning of a new phase in our activities. On Gael's forty-seventh birthday we came together in a small cabin overlooking the Oak Creek Canyon. The location was significant in that it was on the edge of a natural energy anomaly known as a vortex. The location was the same place that Gael and Patrick first stayed when they settled in the area and was the first place that Shelah and I stayed when first visiting our friends there. We met for several hours discussing science, the work ahead for all of us, and our shared concern for the darker directions in which the world was moving. We

52   This was a research project that resulted in the first book published by Earthpulse Press, <u>Angels Don't Play this HAARP: Advances in Tesla Technology</u> by Dr. Nick Begich and Jeane Manning, 1995.

talked about the need to advance science in a direction which empowered individuals.

When science is considered generally it is clear that the technology developed in any given country supports the power of the state. Science, in many instances, becomes the handmaiden of control and power-seeking business and political leaders. Science is released incrementally, suppressed or turned in destructive directions in order to gain control over people or fuel individual lusts for power and money. Science needs to move in a new direction, to serve the individual and free us so we may pursue our greater potentials toward a greater good. The science revealed in these pages is intended to begin that process. The science and new politics which will flow from the synergetic work of our futures is intended to, in some small way, change a bit of our human experience.

During the week we talked about our work and how it would expand and change in the coming years. We are beginning, with deliberate effort, a movement for individual empowerment through delivery of knowledge and technology directly to people. We are not interested in power transfers to governments, politicians or other business leaders. All power in government is derived from the people. All power in business is derived from the consumer. All power in religion is derived from the action of our free will in recognizing the universal power of Spirit.

Towards a New Alchemy; The Millennium Science is about change, new directions and individual empowerment. We look forward to the paths that we construct and then walk down in the coming years. We know that we do not travel alone and shall meet together along the way. We can change the world but we must start by changing ourselves.

Chapter 11

Afterword

The new alchemy is about change and energy transfer. The change is first internal in terms of the individual and then external, finding form in outward expressions. This is the energy transfer, the shifting of focus from internal to external in a modulation of activities.

We are transducers of energy. Transducers change energy from one form to another. Changing energy from one form to another through physical, mental and spiritual activity is what people do. Towards a New Alchemy is about change and recognition of our potency as agents of change. Through our individual and collective "will," reality is altered and transformed. It is creativity at its fullest. In every sense each action and interaction is an alchemy of sorts. It is not some mystery hidden in the caverns of a past age but, rather, it is a vibrant, ongoing process of conscious activity which must only be seen for what it is...creativity.

The recognition of the creative component of our personal interactions is what sets us apart and leads to transformation. Many move through life not seeing the potency of their own spirits which have been blurred behind the fog of daily activities. Creativity is about free exploration of ideas without restraint.

At an early point in my life I studied crystallography as a subset of gemology and geology. In my own study, crystals became a metaphor for life expression. By definition, a crystal is the outward expression of its internal arrangement of atoms. Atoms are the physical expression of smaller particles which are, in turn, the outward expression of energy exchanges. The root of expression is first manifested in energy interactions, hence the metaphor. We begin and are rooted in energy exchanges which take atomic form and then express outwardly in orderly arrangements which becomes our physical manifestation. It can be said that we are the outward expression of our internal arrangement of energy which we transduce into physical form. We are an incredible creative expression as individuals.

Patrick Flanagan's work and creativity has always been focused on increasing understanding of energy. Each of his principals and most significant inventions deal with energy exchanges and transfers. *Towards a New Alchemy* is the crystallization of some of these ideas into written form.

We have moved, in this book, along some of the paths traveled by Drs. Patrick and Gael Crystal Flanagan. Their journey has been one with numerous peaks and plateaus, but the adventure is far from over. Their work is their joy. Their living expression is a clear reflection of their merged spirit. Together they have a vibrant vision for the future.

The most important priority of their current research deals with the continued exploration of the healthful properties of molecularly manipulated water. The research into water has led to the development of products which are beneficial to human health. These technologies represent important work as our industrialized world continues to substitute natural health for the technomaze of complex innovation which continually removes humankind from the earth's created environments. The removal of people from that which is natural has created an artificial and illusionary dependence on things without which we have all come to believe we can not survive. We have become endless consumers having accepted the sales pitch of the corporate world and, in so doing, surrendered much potential. The results of this include incredible levels of human stress which leads to violence, ill health and instabilities. These instabilities impact the individual, family, community and eventually their cumulative force negatively affect the entire planet.

The life goal of Patrick and Gael has been to change the focus of the use of our human potentials from one of dissection and destruction to one of building and coexisting. This is not to suggest that they believe we should all just kind of stand still in some sort of touchy-feely-squishy sort of orgy of happy talk. Quite to the contrary, we are here to find creative expression in all that we do - building up productively without destroying that which is a part of who we are. The idea that we can actualize our creative potentials in all that we do is a hallmark of who we are. We are co-creators on the planet with work to do.

Many people do not see their own creative capacity, but it is inherent in all of us. We all possess a spark of life which manifests in what we do, who we are, and where we go. Every action we take is an outward expression of who we are. We are more than just the reflection in isolated expression. We are more than the compilation of all of our experiences. We are fountains of energy, each person, with the potential for great work. Some will say "but, but, but I don't have the right stuff, the right brain, the right whatever..." The power we are we have now in this very moment. Within this instant, you have the most incredible power of human creativity. The power to choose a course and direction. The power to move your thinking in new ways and the power to change the channel of life's drama. What will you choose?

This last chapter is the crystallization of ideas of a living philosophy which pours out of the lives of the Flanagan's and is an example of what is possible with effort and consideration. It is the idea that technology can serve mankind's higher purposes without dissecting the planet or creating gulfs of separation between people.

Technology should not invade the freedoms of others but add to that freedom...providing greater opportunities for constructive expression.

The inventions offer us all much to enhance our health and life. The Neurophone®, Microclusters®, Air Ionizers and the many other ideas of Flanagan offer us all benefits. In this book we have mentioned but a few of the more interesting ideas Flanagan has developed. There will be more in forthcoming publications of the *Earthpulse Flashpoints* and other publications of the Earthpulse Press.

The Neurophone® is a tool which offers people an opportunity to hear what they otherwise would miss. The same tool offers people the opportunity to control the flow of information into the brain in such a way as to greatly increase their ability to assimilate large amounts of information. The same device may evolve into a linkage for computer to human communications, [53] which could greatly the individual's ability to accumulate information. The ability to take in increased amounts of knowledge will also provide an opportunity to create positive changes in our world. The transfer and global accumulation of knowledge has long since passed the point of rational assimilation by individuals. This acceleration has caused most people to specialize into increasingly narrow knowledge bases. This overspecialization has caused a situation where some of the best minds never have the opportunity to integrate new knowledge across disciplines. The Neurophone® offers an opportunity to increase knowledge across many fields. It will contribute to the new scientist, the new politician, the new thinking, which is solution oriented and recognizes the need to coexist in an increasingly complex world.

Health can be greatly improved using some of Flanagan's technologies. The water research offers a number of possibilities for improving our health and

[53] *Omni* magazine, Date unknown. "The Bionic Brain; Half protoplasm, half circuitry, it's due sooner than we think" by G. Harry Stine, pgs 84-86 & 121-122.

longevity. This work is by no means done. Already a number of new ideas are being developed in Patrick and Gael Crystal Flanagan's lab for additional improvements to this invention. This work will lead to the finest water available to anyone, anywhere.

The opportunity to help change the world in a positive way has always been at the heart of the man, Patrick Flanagan, and is at the heart of all of those around him.

Finally, *Towards a New Alchemy* is about the shift in science. A shift which never ends and is part of an ongoing process. Theories and ideas in science have shifted for thousands of years. Some things found by the ancients of the planet have proven longlasting while others have fallen victim to the advancement of knowledge. Science is for everyone. The advancement of knowledge and willingness to drop old ideas when the facts compel is the essence of the new alchemy. The next millennium is the time when each of us will need to wake up to our more powerful potentials by seeking to do something noble and good for our community and world. It is a time of awakening, questioning and seeking which can only lead to some measure of profound change.

Appendix I

The Neurophone®
How Does it Work?

by Dr. Patrick Flanagan

While investigating man-dolphin communications in the late Sixties, we succeeded in developing a language translator – a device that translated human speech into dolphin language, and visa-versa. A 30 word vocabulary was developed in the project before it ended. This development required a thorough understanding of the nature of speech, and information theory.

First we made many efforts to model the nervous system, and succeeded in demonstrating that the nervous system uses time ratios as major sources of intelligent information. We then began to investigate timing ratios in speech patterns of both humans and dolphins. Through this process, we found that speech intelligibility was contained in time dominant ratios in the speech wave-form. We found that speech quality was contained in dominant frequency ratios. So, the nervous system is designed to recognize two distinct parameters: the time domain, and the frequency domain.

As a result of the knowledge gained in this area, I designed a circuit which suppressed the frequency domain, while amplifying the time domain. This device was so radical in approach that I applied for a patent on it as a specialized speech processor. Six months after the patent was applied for, the National Security Agency (NSA) suppressed my invention under a national security order. My patent application was placed under a secrecy order on August 29, 1968 (order #756,124) by the NSA.

Needless to say I was very disappointed in the patent system. It took four years and three law firms to sue for the release of my invention from this secrecy order. We won the battle, and the secrecy order was rescinded. Patent #3,647,970 was issued on the 7th of March, 1972.

In 1974, two years after I wrote <u>Pyramid Power</u>, I spent the night in the King's Chamber of the Great Pyramid of Giza in Egypt. That night I had an experience of enlightenment, including what is described in Yoga books as a full blown Kundalini Release. It was this awakening experience which helped me connect my speech processing patent to the Neurophone®. It occurred to me that it could be the perfect Neurophone® circuit. When I tried this out, it worked.

The result was the development of the Neurophone® Mk XI which did not require the use of a radio frequency carrier wave. The new Neurophone® worked so well that a voltage of 5 volts generated a signal in the brain that was as loud as the previous device that required a 3,000 volt signal.

The clue as to how the Neurophone® actually works is contained in the skin vibration action which we discovered at Tufts University. The original Neurophone® used a high voltage amplitude modulated carrier wave to create a molecular vibration in the skin itself. The skin became the diaphragm of a biological electrostatic vibrator. The skin is both piezo-electric and opto-electric. That is, when the skin is stimulated by an electric field, or by a photon field, it will contract and vibrate in synchronization with a modulation of the field. If the skin is mechanically stimulated, it will also generate an electric field. In Russia, blind people have been trained to see with their fingertips; and in Czechoslovakia, deaf people have been trained to hear with their fingertips.

The skin is the largest and most complex organ of the living system. As we develop in the womb, all organs of sense perception evolve from the skin. The skin involutes and convolutes to form eyes, ears and other organs of perception. Our research indicates that the skin itself has the latent potential of performing all functions of perception.

The Neurophone® stimulates and makes use of this latent ability. The skin is the organ which receives the signal from the Neurophone®, and converts the incoming signal into a modulated molecular vibration which is then interpreted as sound by the brain. We could theoretically stimulate the sense of sight in a similar way.

We have found that the Neurophone® stimulation also balances the acupuncture meridians, as all acupuncture meridians are present on the surface of the skin,

The Neurophone® converts incoming non-linear acoustic information into a time domain amplified signal. This signal is then transmitted to a pair of high dielectric constant electrodes which are placed in contact with the skin of the head.

The electric field interacts with the skin-electrode combination to create a molecular vibration in the skin which is interpreted by the brain as sound. The result is a new modality for coupling information to the brain, using the skin as the hearing receptor.

Bone conduction vibrators will not work as a Neurophone®, because the mechanical vibratory signal is too gross. The skin must vibrate internally in a synchronous mode in accordance with the time encoded information.

The neural information processing system of the human body is apparently extremely sensitive to time domain information. Doctor Batteau postulated that the nervous system incorporates delay line correlation technology to detect time varied information ratios in a form known as Whitehouse correlation.

The Neurophone® processing circuit processes the incoming complex non-linear audio signal wave-form, and amplifies the non-linearities thus increasing the timing recognition pattern of the signal. In the process, the frequency domain is suppressed. The time-rate-of-change of the incoming signal is thus amplified. This signal is so time dominant, that it can be hard clipped or run through a zero crossing detector without losing any intelligibility.

This time processed signal is then fed to the pair of high dielectric constant electrodes. The signal does not require a radio carrier to work. As stated earlier, the original Neurophone® design had to actually work by brute force, due to the fact that the modulation signal was not processed to increase the time domain signal properties.

As the skin is piezoelectric, and has a dielectric constant in the range of 12,000, the Neurophone® electrodes are made of a ceramic material designed to provide a maximum impedance match to the skin. The entire skin electrode system is a piezoelectric resonator.

Appendix II

Operating Information
The Flanagan Thinkman®

by Dr. Patrick Flanagan

To obtain the best results from your Neurophone® experience, you should spend at least 1/2 hour per day listening to a broad spectrum frequency source in a quiet, relaxing environment. It is best to listen with an increased blood flow to the brain. The preferred position is an inclined plane of 11 degrees with the head down. Testing has shown that most people go into deep alpha within 30 seconds when placed in this position. This state is the most receptive state to listen to the Neurophone®.

The Neurophone® listener can build his own incline plane from a board six feet long, and at least 18 inches wide. The raised end of the board should be supported at a level of 14 inches above the floor.

The electrodes should be placed on the temples, directly behind and slightly above the eyes. Do not place on the hair. Although the electrodes will work perfectly well without electrode jelly, we suggest the use of EEG type electrode jelly, or KY jelly, as this improves impedance matching to the skin.

If you use KY jelly as an electrode cream, smear an even coating over the surface of each electrode, and place the electrodes in contact with the skin.

Later, you may desire to move the electrodes around to experience different sensations. Many Neurophone® listeners prefer to place one electrode in the center of the forehead, on the 3rd eye area, and to place the other one on the back of the neck, or on the hand or wrist.

The sound source for Neurophone® listening can be a cassette player, a radio, or a CD Player. The Neurophone® should be driven from a headphone or a speaker output jack. Your Neurophone® is provided with an audio connector cable with a stereo mini-plug on each end. This will fit most cassette players.

If you want to drive the Neurophone® from another source you may have to obtain a different wire. Your local Radio Shack store will probably have the right one.

In using the Neurophone®, I generally adjust the sound level of the cassette machine to a comfortable listening level as heard through the built in loudspeaker of the machine. I then plug the mini plug into the earphone jack of the player, and plug the standard phone plug into the input jack on the Neurophone®. Plug the electrode phone plug into the Neurophone® electrode output jack.

Rotate the sound source volume control slowly clockwise. Slowly turn the control up until you begin to hear the tape from your cassette player through the Neurophone® electrodes. Depending on the program material to which you are listening, the sound which you first hear through the Neurophone® will not sound very clear.

This is due to two things:

1. The sound you hear is time domain dominant and,

2. As this is a new listening channel, the brain actually has missing signal processing capability.

If we run a frequency sweep of the Neurophone® while listening, we will find that all of us have certain spectra which are entirely missing from our perceptual ability. That is, in the beginning we may hear a complex sound wave of one millisecond duration (1kHz), but miss entirely a sound of another domain. As we listen through the Neurophone® to complex sound information, the missing ranges are programmed into the brain-Neurophone® circuit.

After listening for as little as 30 minutes, the sound begins to take on new qualities. The sound appears to move around in the head, and take on new dimension as we program our psychic brain centers to receive the new signal input. The more the Neurophone® is used, the clearer it gets. I recommend electronic music tapes in the beginning, such as the astral sound tape.

The skin vibration of the new Neurophone® is so great that you may also be able to hear the skin vibrating through your ears. If you are using the Neurophone® as a learning tool this extra brain input can be useful since learning is enhanced by multiple channels into the brain.

Other people in your environment may hear the vibration of your skin as you use the Neurophone®. This is perfectly natural.

In the near future, we will begin to produce cassette tapes and CD's designed to be used only with the Neurophone®. The Neurophonic software tapes will cover many different categories from: Psychic Center Stimulation to Subliminal Learning Programs. We will notify Neurophone® owners as these tapes become available for purchase.

In the beginning, it is not necessary to use special tapes, as the object is to develop the latent channel through which the Neurophone® works. This may be done by listening to white noise (waterfalls) or your favorite music tapes.

Neurophone® stimulated perceptual enhancement increases as you use your Neurophone®. This experience is similar to the meditation experience of transcending. These periods of extreme clarity become more and more pronounced as you put hours on your Neurophone®.

Changes in perceptual awareness are not gradual. Progress is in the form of discrete steps. What may appear to be a gradual altering of consciousness is actually a series of stepped graduations. We may plod along thinking we are making no forward progress, and then, at that point in time where we feel we want to give up, we experience a quantum leap in awareness. One of the most common awareness changes with the Neurophone® effect is an increase in telepathic awareness. Although this cannot be turned on at will, instances of its occurrence will increase in frequency as time goes on.

Please keep a diary of Neurophone® hours of listening, and make note of any change in awareness, dreaming, or unusual perceptual changes. We would like all Neurophone® owners to send us a monthly research report or diary of experiences. This is important data which will enable us to share with you all experiences, and fine tune the Neurophone® experience. Keep note of your actual listening time, and listening material. If you experience any change in consciousness or awareness please write it down. Others would like to share your experience.

It may be possible to make a mind-link between two or more people by using Neurophone® technology. We have experimented with this process and believe that it may be possible to learn directly from the mind of another person by means of a Neurophone® mind-link. We have succeeded in creating mind links on several occasions. This may be a promising area for future Neurophone® research. The technique may be best accomplished by using computerized Neurophone®s which are in the process of development.

This linking could be done in a number of ways. The Soviets had established that an EEG machine of only 16 channels could pick up the entire consciousness of an individual. All that is then necessary is to feed the data into the mind of another by means of a multi-channel Neurophone®. The Neurophone® would then become an electronic corpus collosum between the minds of two or more people. The corpus collosum is the brain bridge which links the two sides of the brain. The Neurophone® becomes this bridge between two people, a new medium for communications linkages.

Appendix III

Quick Start
The Flanagan Thinkman®

by Dr. Patrick Flanagan

The Flanagan Neurophone® consists of a signal processing box with an on/off switch, an input jack and an electrode output jack.

The Flanagan Neurophone® does not come with a battery. Before using the device open the Flanagan Neurophone® box by removing the two screws which are in the bottom of the device. Carefully lift off the top of the box and connect a standard 9 volt alkaline battery to the battery clip provided found inside. Close the box and replace the screws. You are now ready to use the Flanagan Neurophone®.

Any audio source can be used with the device. A tape player, CD player or other sound generating device needs to be connected to the Flanagan Neurophone®. There is a 1/8" connection cable provided with the device. Connect the cable to the stereo headphone output jack on the tape or CD player. Connect the other end of the cable to the receptacle marked "In" on the Flanagan Neurophone®. Make sure the audio volume control on the tape or CD player is turned down when starting up the device. The electrode headset provided with the Flanagan Neurophone® is then connected to the receptacle on the device which is marked "Out".

Wet the electrodes with tap water or KY Jelly and apply the electrodes to the temples of the head right behind the eyes. Make sure the electrodes touch the skin and that hair is not trapped between the skin and the electrodes. In order for the Neurophone® to work properly, the electrodes must touch the skin.

Turn the switch located on the back of the Flanagan Neurophone® to the "on" position. A dull glow from the light emitting diode on the front panel of the Neurophone® will signal that the device is working and that the battery is providing power.

Slowly turn the volume control of the tape or CD player up until the sound is heard comfortably through the Flanagan Neurophone®. Turn the volume up to the point where the sound becomes distorted and then turn it down until it is clear and loud. The signal may not be very loud initially.

Use the device one hour a day for a week. During the week the signal will increase in clarity and volume. At the end of this first period of use the volume will reach a 95% volume efficiency level for the individual user. Keep in mind that the signal although weak initially will strengthen during this period of time. Also, remember that sometimes no signal is heard when the device is activated and it may take up to an hour before the first sound is noticed (this is common when deaf persons and others have first used the Flanagan Neurophone®).

Since the Flanagan Neurophone® works through the skin, it is important not to try and "hear" through the ears. As you relax and pay attention to the Flanagan Neurophone® signal, you will develop the ability to hear through your skin. As the skin pathway is developed, the signal will "fill out" in frequency response and your sensitivity to the device will increase. It is helpful when first using the device to plug your ears so that the focus on the internal hearing can be reinforced.

Note on the Electrodes: Do not try to pry the piezo-elements off of the electrodes. This will damage the unit and void the warranty. Do not touch the metal electrodes together for an extended time. This could also damage the electrodes. When the electrodes are in contact with the skin, an electronic circuit is completed that makes the skin a part of a piezo-electric circuit in which the electrodes and skin vibrate. The Flanagan Neurophone® works by causing a vibration in the skin. People who are next to you will be able to hear your skin vibrate in accordance with the Flanagan Neurophone® signal.

Let us know what you experience. We appreciate the feedback of users as this increases all of our knowledge of the various ways which the Flanagan Neurophone® can be used.

Enjoy the first generation of the Millennium sound.

Appendix IV

Partial List of Dr. Patrick Flanagan's Inventions

This is a partial listing of some of Dr. Flanagan's over three hundred inventions. In the future, the availability of these technologies will be announced in the *Earthpulse Flashpoints.*

3D Sound System
Bio-Energy Measuring Device
Brain Entrainment Device
Chakra Detector and Mapper
Color Sonar System
Copper Microclusters®
Crystal Energy® concentrate
Cubit Wand Exercise System
Diver Communications Transceiver
Dolphin-Man Communications System
Earth Resonance Generator
Electron Cascade Air Purifier
Electronic Sleep Machine
ELF Detection System for Earth Waves
Gold Microclusters®
Guided Missile Detector
Hydrogen Negative Ion Detector
Infrared Bio Entrainment - Circular Polarized
Infrared Brain Circulation Enhancement

Infrared Electronic Signature Detector

Infrared Heating Device - Long Wave

Infrared Scanning Device

Ion Generator

Laser Microphone

Man Dolphin Communicator/Translator

Manganese Microclusters®

Neurophone® Direct Brain Communications Device

Nutrient Delivery System

Packet Radio Communications

Pharmaceutical Delivery System

Pink Noise Neurophone®

Rubidium Microclusters®

Secret Communications Device

Sonic Dolphin Echo Location Device

Scalar Wave Bioentrainment Device

Scalar Wave Receiver

Scalar Wave Transmitter

Scalar Under Water Communicator

Scalar Through the Earth Communications

Sensor® I

Sensor® II

Sensor® III

Silica Microclusters®

Silver Microclusters®

Sonic Dolphin Human Echo Location Device

Classified Secret:Voice Scrambler Time Ratio Encoding

Tensor Wave through the Earth Communicator

Titanium Microclusters®

Zero Phase Shift Audio Frequency Filter

Zinc Microclusters®

Appendix V

Dr. Patrick Flanagan's Inventions

The Neurophone® and Electro Field Generator Patents

United States Patent [19]

Flanagan

[11] Patent Number: 4,743,275

[45] Date of Patent: May 10, 1988

[54] ELECTRON FIELD GENERATOR

[76] Inventor: G. Patrick Flanagan, P.O. Box 2285, Sedona, Ariz. 86336

[21] Appl. No.: 899,713

[22] Filed: Aug. 25, 1986

[51] Int. Cl.⁴ B03C 3/12; B03C 3/41
[52] U.S. Cl. 55/2; 55/123;
55/138; 55/150; 361/226; 361/230

[58] Field of Search 55/2, 123, 146, 150,
55/155, 138; 361/225, 226, 230, 231

[56] References Cited

U.S. PATENT DOCUMENTS

2,085,735	7/1937	Brion et al.	55/150 X
2,086,063	7/1937	Brion et al.	55/123
2,239,694	4/1941	Bennett	361/230 X
2,958,393	11/1960	Lueder	55/155
3,403,252	9/1968	Nagy	361/231
3,417,302	12/1968	Lueder	55/2 X
3,789,278	1/1974	Bingham et al.	361/230 X
3,970,905	7/1976	Itoh et al.	55/146 X
4,037,268	7/1977	Gallagher	55/150 X
4,096,544	6/1978	Ignatjev	361/231
4,391,773	7/1983	Flanagan	55/2 X

Primary Examiner—Kathleen J. Prunner
Attorney, Agent, or Firm—Edmond T. Patnaude

[57] **ABSTRACT**

A negative field generator has a dielectric slab which is doped with discrete conductive members and sandwiched between a pair of electrodes. The electrodes and the dielectric member are encapsulated in a dielectric material and the electrodes are connected across a source of high frequency high A.C. voltage.

13 Claims, 1 Drawing Sheet

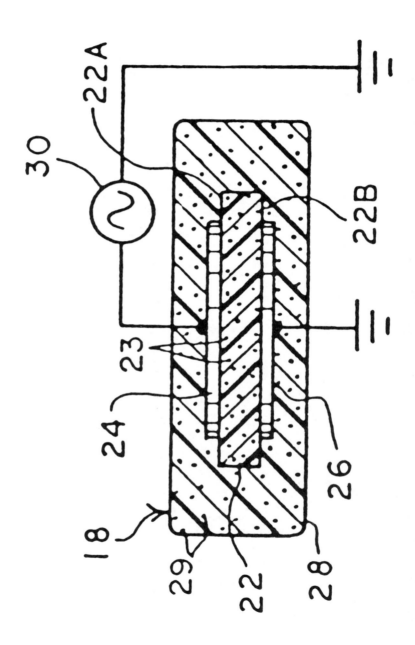

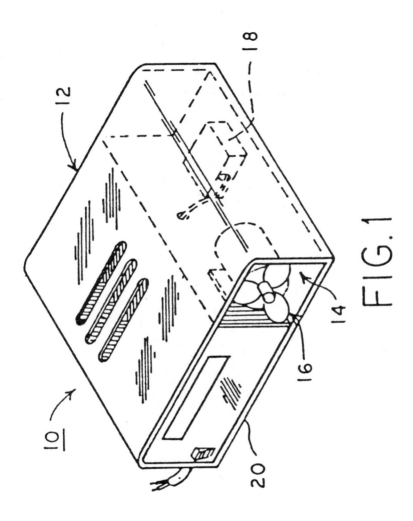

FIG. 1

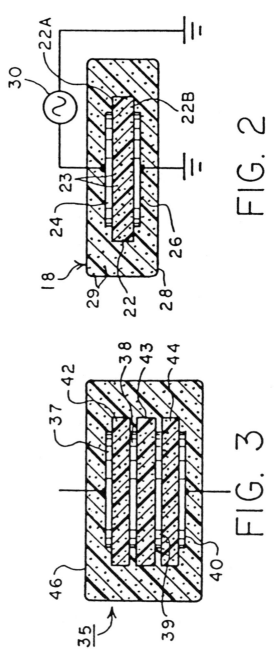

FIG. 2

FIG. 3

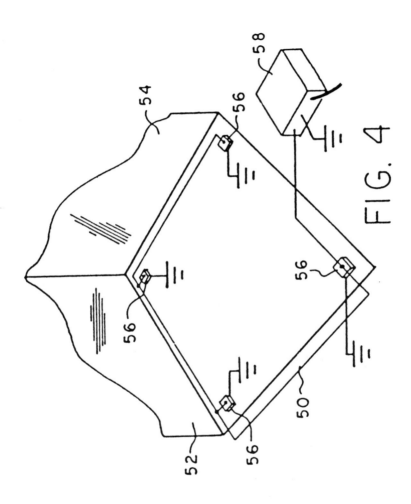

FIG. 4

4,743,275

1

ELECTRON FIELD GENERATOR

The present invention relates in general to a new and improved device and method for generating a negative electric field of sufficient intensity to purify air, and it also relates to a novel method of enhancing the field strength of an electric field generator.

BACKGROUND OF THE INVENTION

In U.S. Pat. No. 4,391,773 there is described a negative field generator having utility in the purification of air. The generator which is described in that patent includes a field emitting device in the form of a flat solid dielectric material on the opposite faces of which a pair of electrodes are respectively disposed. When a high frequency, high voltage source is connected across the electrodes, a high intensity, high frequency negative field is developed in the space surrounding the field emitting device, and this negative field causes airborne solids to precipitate out of the surrounding air.

SUMMARY OF THE INVENTION

Briefly, in accordance with the teachings of the present invention the strength of the negative field generated by the above-described prior art field emitter is advantageously affected by altering the composition of the dielectric. I have found that if the dielectric material is doped with conductive or semiconductive particles the strength of the field produced externally of the field emitter is greatly increased.

In accordance with another aspect of the present invention, a plurality of the novel field emitters of the

2

velocity electric fan 16 is mounted in the tunnel near the front end thereof to cause the ambient air to flow into the front end and out the back end of the tunnel. A negative electric field emitter 18 is mounted to the floor 20 of the cabinet 12 within the tunnel 14 so that the air flowing through the tunnel passes through the negative electric field which surrounds the field emitter 18 which is confined by the grounded metal walls of the tunnel.

As the air flows through the tunnel 14 it is thus treated by the high frequency, high energy negative field which surrounds the field emitter 18.

As discussed above, solid matter carried by the air is precipitated by the negative field and if desired, a porous filter (not shown) may be placed over the rear end of the tunnel to collect the precipitated particles before they leave the tunnel. Otherwise, as tests have shown, the precipitated particles will drop to the floor in the vicinity of the device 10.

Another use of the device 10 is in the conversion of carbon monoxide to carbon dioxide as carbon monoxide gas is passed through the tunnel 14. Also the electric charge on material located a substantial distance from the device 10 has been altered by the air exiting the tunnel 14. In this latter case the use of the device 10 in a pillow manufacturing plant caused pieces of foam filler which had previously clung to the walls and ceilings of the area to fall to the floor where they were then easily swept up. The device 10 also works well as a deodorizer.

Referring to FIG. 2, the field emitter 18 may be seen to comprise a slab or sheet 22 of a solid dielectric material such as glass, paraffin, acrylic, epoxy or other suitable dielectric in which a plurality of small particles or present invention can be strategically located in a room or other area to purify the air in the room without the need for auxiliary means for circulating the air in the room past the field emitters. Also, a plurality of the novel field emitters can be stacked on one another and connected in series across the high frequency, high voltage source to increase the strength of the negative field developed around the emitter.

GENERAL DESCRIPTION OF THE DRAWINGS

The present invention will be better understood by a reading of the following detailed description taken in connection with the accompanying drawing wherein:

FIG. 1 is a perspective view of an air purifier embodying the novel negative field generator of the present invention;

FIG. 2 is a cross-sectional view of a negative field generator embodying a novel field emitter constructed in accordance with the teachings of the present invention;

FIG. 3 is a cross-sectional view of another field emitter embodying the present invention; and

FIG. 4 is a schematic illustration of still another embodiment of the invention.

DETAILED DESCRIPTION OF A PREFERRED EMBODIMENT

Referring to FIG. 1, there is shown a metal housing or cabinet 12 in which is mounted an electronic control unit including a high voltage, high frequency power supply having a voltage of at least 5000 volts and a frequency of at least 20 kiloHertz. A passageway or tunnel 14 connected to the power supply is located at one side of the cabinet and is surrounded by the metal cabinet, which itself is connected to ground. A low

granules 23 of conductive or semiconductive material are dispersed. A pair of planar electrodes 24 and 26 are mounted to the opposite faces 22A and 22B of the member 22 to form a capacitor which may be encapsulated in an insulator 28. The member 22 is square when viewed from the top as are the electrodes 24 and 26, but these members may, if desired, be circular or of some other suitable shape. The corresponding dimensions of the dielectric member are greater than those of the electrodes 24 and 26. The insulator 28 is also a solid dielectric material such as glass, paraffin, acrylic, epoxy or other suitable dielectric and may be doped so as to include conductive or semiconductive particles or granules 29 dispersed therein.

As shown, the electrode 24 is connected to one terminal of a high voltage, high frequency source of electric energy 30, and the electrode 26 is connected via ground to the other terminal of the energy source 30. The voltage applied across the emitter has a frequency of at least 20 kiloHertz and a voltage of at least 5000 volts RMS.

The reason why the field strength is increased by the presence of conductive particles in the dielectric material is not fully understood. However, comparative tests have proven that the electric field is strengthened and significantly improved air purification is achieved when such materials are dispersed in the dielectric, and it is believed that the work function of the dielectric is altered by the added material and this results in the increased emission from the device.

Referring to FIG. 3, there is shown a negative electric field emitter 35 which comprises a plurality of planar metallic electrodes 37, 38, 39 and 40 separated by a plurality of flat dielectric members 42, 43 and 44. The electrodes and the dielectric members are encapsulated in an insulating material 46. Conductive leads extend

3

4,743,275

from the electrodes 37 and 40 through the insulating material 46 for connection of the field emitter 35 to a high frequency, high voltage source to develop a generally toroidal electric field around the field emitter 35.

Referring to FIG. 4 there is shown in schematic form the floor 50 and two side walls 52 and 54 of a room. Four field emitters 56 are mounted on the floor near the four corners of the room and are electrically connected to a power supply 58 to apply a high frequency high voltage across each of the field emitters 56. For convenience of installation, one terminal of each of the emitters 56 is grounded and the other terminals are connected to the hot terminal of the power supply 58. The field emitters may be of the type shown in FIG. 2 or of the type shown in FIG. 3 and the power supply 58 provides an output of at least 5000 volts RMS at a frequency of at least 20 kiloHertz. By strategically locating the field emitters 56 within the room the need for fans for circulating the air through the electric fields surrounding the emitters can be eliminated thereby reducing the initial cost and the operating cost of the system as well as the noise associated with such fans.

In order to substantiate the fact that doping of the insulator with different non-dielectric materials alters the resultant field and in some cases increases the field strength a substantial amount, several different experiments were conducted. In making these experiments, three different emitters of identical size and shape were constructed. The dielectric slabs were circular being 80

4

parting from the true spirit and scope of the present invention. Therefore, it is intended by the appended claims to cover all such changes and modifications which come within the true spirit and scope of this invention.

What is claimed:

1. Apparatus for generating an electric field of the type comprising a solid dielectric member sandwiched between first and second electrodes and a high voltage, high frequency energy source connected between said electrodes, the improvement wherein said dielectric member comprises,

a dielectric material having a plurality of discrete, conductive members dispersed therein.

2. Apparatus according to claim 1 wherein said conductive members are semiconductive.

3. Apparatus according to claim 2 wherein said conductive members are formed of silicon carbide.

4. Apparatus according to claim 2 wherein said conductive members are silicon carbide granules randomly dispersed in said dielectric material.

5. Apparatus according to claim 4 wherein said dielectric material is parafinic.

6. Apparatus according to claim 1 wherein said conductive members are paramagnetic.

7. Apparatus according to claim 6 wherein said dielectric material is parafinic.

mm in diameter and 15 mm thick. The plates were 63 mm in diameter. In one emitter, the dielectric was a pure epoxy. In a second emitter the dielectric was epoxy containing ten percent by volume of small lead spheres dispersed throughout the epoxy so as to be insulated from one another. The spheres had a diameter of 0.7 mm. In a third emitter the epoxy was doped with silicon carbide granules having a size of 75 mesh. These granules were of the type used in lapidary grinding and thus contain a substantial amount of elemental impurities wherefor the material is actually a crude semi-conductor. It is also paramagnetic.

The emitters were connected across a high frequency power supply of 24 kV at 44 kiloHertz in the manner described in my U.S. Pat. No. 4,391,773 using a Kiethly Elecrometer and an ion/electron probe. At a distance of ten centimeters from the emitters the following measurements were made.

Pure epoxy dielectric	2.98×10^{11} electrons/cm²
Epoxy with lead spheres	3.97×10^{11} electrons/cm²
Epoxy with silicon carbide	4.76×10^{11} electrons/cm²

It may thus be seen that the addition of conductive or semiconducive or paramagnetic particles to the dielectric greatly increases the field strength of the field generated by the emitter.

While the present invention has been described in connection with particular embodiments thereof, it will be understood by those skilled in the art that many changes and modifications may be made without de-

8. A method of purifying air, comprising the steps of: placing in proximity to said air a capacitor including a pair of electrodes spaced apart by a solid dielectric material in which a plurality of mutually spaced apart conductive pieces are dispersed, applying between said electrodes an A.C. voltage of at least 5000 volts having a frequency of at least 20 kiloHertz.

9. A method according to claim 8 wherein said capacitor is encapsulated in a solid insulating material.

10. A method according to claim 9 wherein a plurality of members selected from the group of conductive and semiconductive materials are dispersed in said insulating material.

11. A method of purifying the air in an environmental area, comprises the steps of placing at respectively spaced locations in said area a plurality of capacitors each having first and second spaced electrodes separated by a solid dielectric member formed of a dielectric material in which a plurality of conductive pieces are dispersed, and connecting between the associated ones of said first and second spaced electrodes an A.C. voltage of at least 5000 volts and having a frequency of at least 20 kiloHertz.

12. A method according to claim 11 wherein said pieces are semiconductive.

13. A method acording to claim 11 wherein said pieces are paramagnetic.

* * * * *

United States Patent Office

3,393,279

Patented July 16, 1968

1

3,393,279

NERVOUS SYSTEM EXCITATION DEVICE

Gillis Patrick Flanagan, Bellaire, Tex., assignor to Listening Incorporated, Arlington, Mass., a corporation of Massachusetts

Filed Mar. 13, 1962, Ser. No. 179,337,

3 Claims. (Cl. 179—107)

This invention relates to electromagnetic excitation of the nervous system of a mammal and pertains more particularly to a method and apparatus for exciting the nervous system of a person with electromagnetic waves that are capable of causing that person to become conscious of information conveyed by the electromagnetic waves.

It is an object of the present invention to provide a means of initiating controllable responses of the neuro senses without applying pressure waves or stress waves to the ears or bones. Another object of this invention is to provide a means of causing a person to receive an aural perception of the sound corresponding to the audio modulation of radio frequency electromagnetic waves that are coupled with the nervous system of the person. These and other objects of this invention will be understood from the following drawings and description of the invention, wherein:

FIGURE 1 is a schematic illustration of one form of the present nervous system excitation device.

FIGURE 2 is a circuit diagram of one form of the present nervous system excitation device.

FIGURE 3 is a diagrammatic view illustrating one form of field generator adapted to be used with the device of FIGURE 1.

2

in which the noise level is high, as a device by which a person can listen to an audio signal that cannot be heard by others, etc.

As shown in FIGURE 1 of the drawing, in a preferred form of the invention, a field of electromagnetic waves is generated by a field generating means, such as a pair of electrodes 1. The electrodes 1 are preferably electrically insulated, for example by surrounding them with a suitable electrical insulating material 2, and are arranged to generate a field coupled with at least a portion of the nervous system of a person, for example by being placed near or along opposite sides of a person's head. The electrodes 1 can be placed in direct contact with the skin and the electrodes can be placed on or near various portions of the body, such portions preferably being near the spinal cord.

The electrodes 1 are electrically connected to a source of modulated electromagnetic waves inclusive of a radio frequency power amplifier and variable frequency oscillator, indicated in box 3, an audio modulator, indicated in box 4, a source of audio signal, indicated in box 5, and a power supply for the signal source, modulator and amplifier, indicated in box 6. The variable frequency oscillator 3 is preferably provided with a manual radio frequency control means, indicated by box 3a. Numerous forms of the components, indicated in boxes 3 to 6, that provide suitable power and a source of modulated electromagnetic waves are presently known and the known devices can suitably be used as long as they are arranged to produce a relatively high voltage output that has a radio frequency above the audio range and is capable of being modulated by an audio signal or other signal adapted to

FIGURE 4 is a diagrammatic view illustrating another form of field generator adapted to be used with the device of FIGURE 1.

The present invention involves the discovery that certain electromagnetic waves induce responses in the nervous systems of mammals. In human beings a response is produced when some or all of a person's nervous system is placed within a field of electromagnetic waves having a radio frequency above the audible range. In addition, when the nervous system of a person is contacted by modulated electromagnetic carrier waves of such a frequency, the nervous system is responsive to the modulation of the carrier waves. Each individual nervous system is at least somewhat selective in respect to the frequencies to which it is most responsive. A frequency to which the nervous system of a person is demonstrably responsive can be determined by varying the frequency of carrier waves that are modulated by an information signal, such as speech or music, and measuring the frequency of such waves that produce the sensation of hearing the sounds corresponding to the modulating signal.

In the method of the present invention, a response is initiated in the nervous system of a mammal by disposing at least a portion of that nervous system within a field of electromagnetic waves of a radio frequency above the aural range. In a preferred embodiment of this invention, the field to which the nervous system is exposed is a field containing modulated electromagnetic waves of a particular radio frequency to which the individual nervous system is selectively responsive. In a particularly preferred embodiment of this invention, at least a portion of the nervous system of a person is exposed to audio modulated electromagnetic waves having a radio frequency such that the person experiences the sensation of hearing, substantially free of distortion, the information which is conveyed by the audio modulation.

The present invention may be used as a hearing aid, as an aid to teaching speech to a person who was born deaf, as a means of communicating with persons in locations

be conveyed by the modulation of electromagnetic waves of such a frequency.

The modulation can suitably be effected by means of either an amplitude or frequency modulation of such electromagnetic waves. These waves preferably have a frequency in the range of from about 20 kilocycles per second to about 200 kilocycles per second. The output of the source of modulated electromagnetic waves is preferably at least about 1 watt where the field generator comprises a pair of insulated electrodes placed on the head of a person. The extent to which a person is aurally perceptive to the output supplied at a given wattage is materially increased when at least one of the electrodes is placed in electrical contact with the body of the person.

In a preferred mode of operating the apparatus shown in FIGURE 1, the electrodes 1 are placed on the sides of the head of a person. The source 5 of audio signal is actuated to produce an audio signal corresponding to sounds recognizable by that person, and source 3 of modulated electromagnetic waves is actuated to couple the waves with the nervous system of that person. When control 3A is adjusted so that the frequency of the modulated waves is a frequency to which his nervous system is particularly responsive, the person to whom the field of such waves is applied has the sensation of hearing the sounds corresponding to the audio signal substantially free of distortion.

In the circuit shown in FIGURE 2, a phase shift type of carrier oscillator, generally designated by dotted rectangle 7, with a frequency control, generally designated by rectangle 8, is arranged to produce electromagnetic waves, shown at A, a frequency ranging from about 20 to about 200 kilocycles per second. The oscillator output is coupled through capacitor 9 to a radio frequency power amplifier, generally designated by dotted rectangle 10. Potentiometer 11, which is connected between capacitor 9 and ground, provides a means of adjusting the input to the amplifier. Switch 12, which is connected to the cathode of tube 13 of the amplifier, provides a means

3

of switching between resistors 14 and 15 to vary the operating power characteristics of the tube.

The output of amplifier 10 is connected to transformer 16 which is coupled back-to-back with transformer 17. This arrangement of transformers provides an inductive load such that the amplifier yields a high voltage output and is isolated from other components of the circuit. Resistor 18 connected across the output side of transformer 17 serves to reduce any dangerous voltage spikes which might be produced. The output side of transformer 17 is connected to a suitable field generator, which may comprise the electrodes 1 surrounded by insulating material 2.

The output of amplifier 10 is amplitude modulated by means of the modulator generally designated by dotted rectangle 19. A fluctuating electrical signal B, preferably of audio frequency, is applied to the modulator by means of input jack 20 and transformer 21. The output of the modulator varies the screen voltage of tube 13 of the amplifier so that the modulation envelope of the current oscillation C produced across the load of tube 13 correspond to the fluctuating signal B applied to the modulator.

Potentiometer 22 is connected to the cathode of tube 23 as the cathode resistor of tube 23. Potentiometer 22 is preferably adjusted so that the plate current of tube 13 is about half its normal maximum value. The fluctuating signal applied to modulator 19 is then adjusted to cause the plate current of tube 13 to vary between the maximum and minimum values so that a large current variation occurs in the load 16 of tube 13.

The apparatus shown in FIGURE 2 has been used to

4

generating means which is adapted to be placed around the head of a person.

It is to be understood that the above embodiments and examples have been presented for descriptive purposes and that, within the scope of the appended claims, the invention may be practiced otherwise than specifically illustrated and described.

I claim:

1. A method of transmitting audio information to the brain of a subject through the nervous system of the subject which method comprises, in combination, the steps of generating a radio frequency signal having a frequency in excess of the highest frequency of the audio information to be transmitted, modualting said radio frequency signal with the audio information to be transmitted, and applying said modulated radio frequency signal to a pair of insulated electrodes and placing both of said insulated electrode in physical contact with the skin of said subject, the strength of said radio frequency electromagnetic field being high enough at the skin surface to cause the sensation of hearing the audio information modulated thereon in the brain of said subject and low enough so that said subject experiences no physical discomfort.

2. The method of claim 1 wherein said modulated electromagnetic field is coupled with a portion of the nervous system contained in the person's spinal column.

3. Apparatus for transmitting audio information to the brain of a subject through the nervous system of the subject comprising, in combination, means for generating a radio frequency signal having a frequency greater than the maximum frequency of said audio information, means for modulating said radio frequency signal with the audio

communicate speech and music to numerous persons-including registered physicians. In these uses the electrodes 1, in the form of circular disc covered by a plastic insulation 2, were placed against the sides of the heads of the persons. When the electromagnetic waves were adjusted to a frequency to which persons having normal hearing were selectively responsive, none of these persons perceived any sensations of hearing or experienced any discomfort when no audio modulation was applied to the waves. When the waves were audio modulated with a speech or music signal, none of these persons experienced any discomfort, but they each had the sensation of listening to the transmitted information and "hearing" it at least as clearly as they would hear such information from an audible transmitter. When the same apparatus was similarly employed on a person whose hearing had been damaged to an extent requiring a hearing aid to hear normal conversation, that person "heard" the audio signal (with this hearing aid disconnected) and "heard" music with a better fidelity than that obtainable with his hearing aid.

FIGURE 3 shows an arrangement for mounting the field generating means in a position such that a portion of a person's nervous system may be moved into and out of coupling with the field at the will of the person. In this arrangement, electrodes 1 surrounded by insulation 2 are mounted in vertical alignment along the back of a seating device, such as chair 24. When a person is seated and leaning back in the chair, portions of his nervous system are brought into coupling relationship with the field produced by electrodes 1.

FIGURE 4 shows an alternative arrangement of the field generating means. In this arrangement, inductive coil 25 is connected to the output of a suitable source of modulated electromagnetic waves and serves as a field

information to be transmitted, electrode means adapted to generate a localized radio frequency electromagnetic field thereabout when excited by a radio frequency signal, and means coupling said modulated radio frequency signal to said electrode means, said electrode means having a surface adapted to be capacitively coupled to a localized area at the surface of the skin of said subject when placed in physical contact therewith whereby said electrode means may generate a localized radio frequency electromagnetic field modulated by said audio information at the surface of the skin of said subject, and means on said surface of said electrode means for insulating said electrode means from the skin of said subject.

References Cited

UNITED STATES PATENTS

3,170,993	2/1965	Puharich et al. -----	179—107
1,001,236	8/1911	Bachelet ------------	128—1.5
1,120,964	12/1914	Neel ---------------	128—1.5
2,004,751	6/1935	Fischer -----------	128—423 X
2,103,440	12/1937	Weissenberg --------	128—1.3
2,118,594	5/1938	Dowden ------------	128—1.5 X
2,438,605	3/1948	Hart --------------	128—1.5 X
2,713,120	7/1955	Mostofsky ---------	128—423 X
1,735,267	11/1929	Eichhorn ---------	179—107
2,995,633	8/1961	Puhdrich ---------	179—107

OTHER REFERENCES

Rutschmann, pp. 22, 23, IRE Transactions on Med. Electronics, March 1959.

KATHLEEN H. CLAFFY, *Primary Examiner.*
ROBERT H. ROSE, *Examiner.*
J. W. JOHNSON, A. A. McGILL, *Assistant Examiners.*

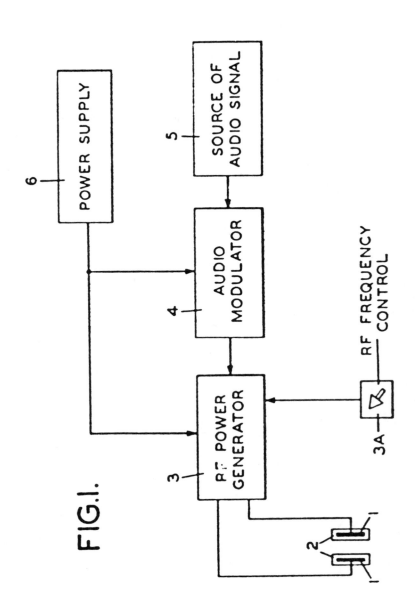

FIG.1.

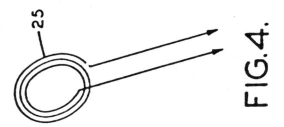

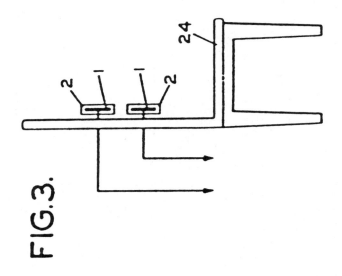

FIG.4.

FIG.3.

July 16, 1968   G. P. FLANAGAN   3,393,279

NERVOUS SYSTEM EXCITATION DEVICE

Filed March 13, 1962   2 Sheets—Sheet 2

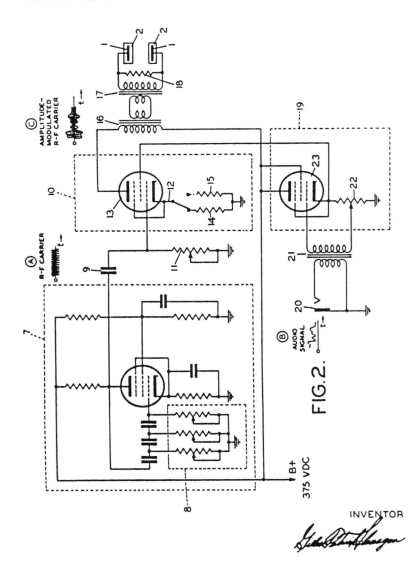

FIG.2.

INVENTOR

United States Patent

Flanagan

[15] **3,647,970**

[45] **Mar. 7, 1972**

[54] **METHOD AND SYSTEM FOR SIMPLIFYING SPEECH WAVEFORMS**

[72] Inventor: **Gillis P. Flanagan**, 5207 Mimosa, Bellaire, Tex. 77401

[22] Filed: **Aug. 29, 1968**

[21] Appl. No.: **756,124**

[52] U.S. Cl. ....179/1.5, 179/1.5 M, 179/1.5 E, 325/32, 328/31

[51] Int. Cl. H04k 1/00

[58] Field of Search ....179/1.5 MS, 1.5 E, 15.55, 1 AS; 340/15.5 FC; 328/31; 307/237

[56] **References Cited**

UNITED STATES PATENTS

2,479,338	8/1949	Gabrilovitch	179/1.5
2,953,644	9/1960	Miller	179/15.55
2,979,611	4/1961	Halina	179/15.55

Primary Examiner—Rodney D. Bennett, Jr.
Assistant Examiner—H. A. Birmiel
Attorney—Richards, Harris & Hubbard

[57] **ABSTRACT**

A speech waveform is converted to a constant amplitude square wave in which the transitions between the amplitude extremes are spaced so as to carry the speech information. The system includes a pair of tuned amplifier circuits which act as high-pass filters having a 6 decibel per octave slope from 0 to 15,000 cycles followed by two stages, each comprised of an amplifier and clipper circuit, for converting the filtered waveform to a square wave. A radio transmitter and receiver having a plurality of separate channels within a conventional single side band transmitter bandwidth and a system for transmitting secure speech information are also disclosed.

19 Claims, 4 Drawing Figures

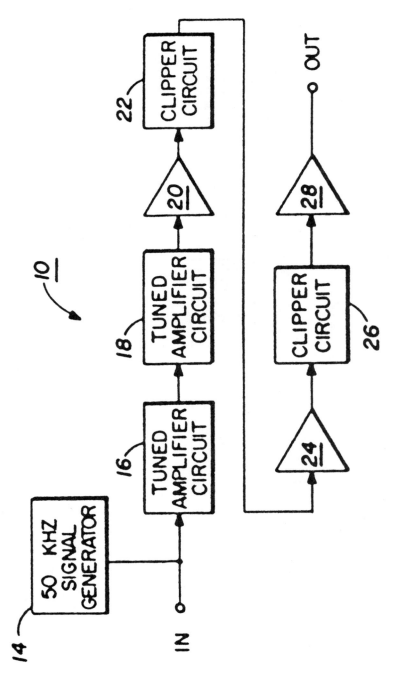

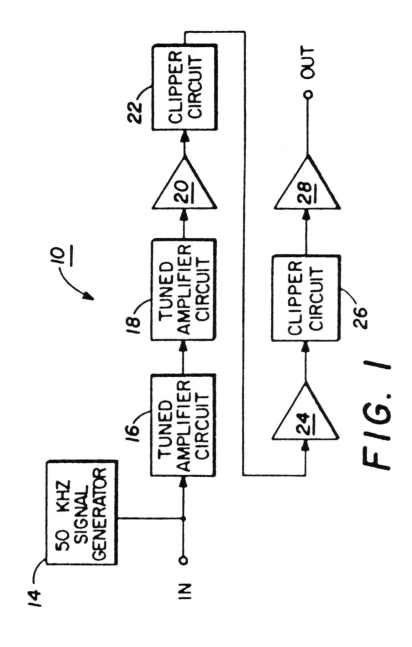

FIG. 1

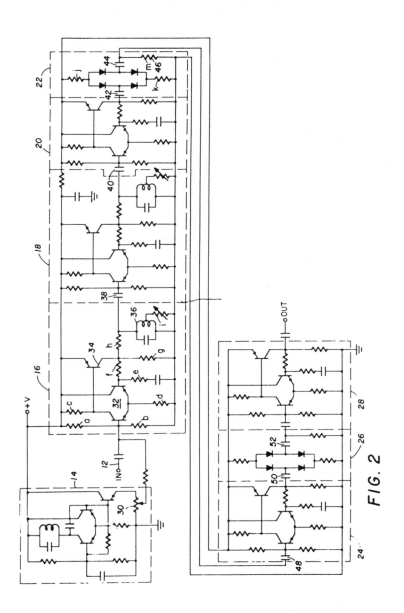

FIG. 2

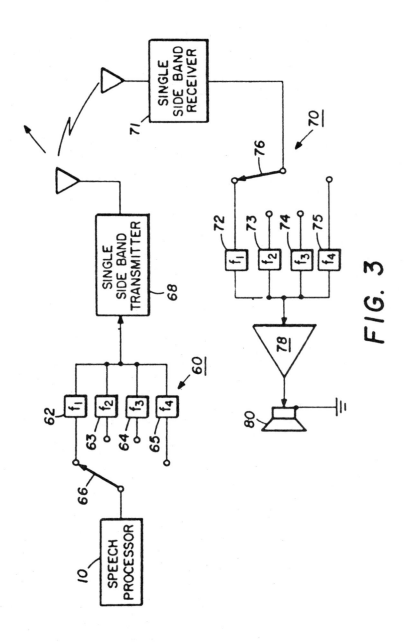

FIG. 3

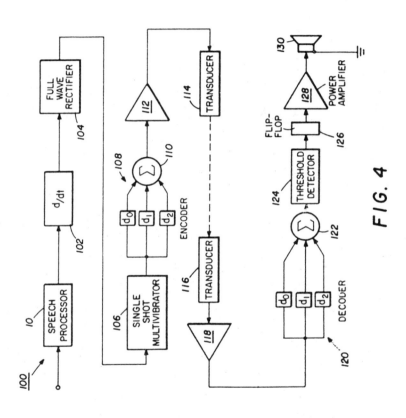

FIG. 4

1

METHOD AND SYSTEM FOR SIMPLIFYING SPEECH
WAVEFORMS

BACKGROUND OF INVENTION

This invention relates generally to electronic processing of speech, and more particularly relates to a method and system for simplifying the speech waveform to facilitate transmission of the speech through various media without materially degrading intelligibility.

In the process of producing human speech, the voice box creates a series of sound pulses which reverberate within and are shaped by the upper throat and mouth cavity. The frequency of the pulses produced by the voice box primarily determines the frequency or pitch of the sound, while the shape of the mouth cavity reverberates and shapes the sound pulses to produce the speech information. The resulting speech waveform is very complex and highly redundant. If such a waveform is passed through a band-pass filter having a bandwidth significantly less than 3,000 cycles per second, the speech becomes unintelligible. Thus, even the simplest voice communication channels require a substantial bandwidth. Heretofore it has been commonly believed that the speech information was contained in the amplitude as well as the frequency modulation of the speech waveform. When voice sounds are induced in a body of water or the earth, the many reverberations caused by the various velocity discontinuities make speech unintelligible over relatively short transmission lengths. Also, the complex speech waveform has made encoding or scrambling for secure transmissions, either by electromagnetic, electrical, or pressure waves, so impractical as to be very seldom used.

SUMMARY OF INVENTION CLAIMED

This invention is concerned with a method and system for simplifying a complex speech waveform so that it can be used

2

transmitter. The receiver has similar narrow band-pass filters so as to be selectively sensitive to transmissions in that pass band.

In accordance with another specific aspect of the invention, each transition of the square wave is converted to a pulse of predetermined amplitude and width, which is then converted into a plurality of pulses with predetermined time spacing. These pulses are then transmitted to a receiver where the plurality of spaced pulses are recombined as one pulse. The square wave is then reproduced from the recombined pulses.

BRIEF DESCRIPTION OF THE DRAWINGS

The novel features believed characteristic of this invention are set forth in the appended claims. The invention itself, however, as well as other objects and advantages thereof, may best be understood by reference to the following detailed description of illustrative embodiments, when read in conjunction with the accompanying drawings, wherein:

FIG. 1 is a schematic block diagram of a system for processing a simplified speech waveform in accordance with the present invention;

FIG. 2 is a detailed schematic circuit diagram of the system of FIG. 1;

FIG. 3 is a schematic block diagram of a multichannel transmitter in accordance with the present invention; and

FIG. 4 is a schematic block diagram of a system for transmitting and receiving scrambled speech waveforms in accordance with the present invention.

DESCRIPTION OF PREFERRED EMBODIMENTS

Referring now to the drawings, and in particular to FIG. 1, a speech processor in accordance with the present invention is indicated generally by the reference numeral 10. The speech waveform is applied to the input 12 as a voltage signal derived for a multitude of applications. The simplified speech waveform may be passed through a narrow band-pass filter, thus permitting a greater number of communication channels within a given frequency band. The simplified speech waveform can be transmitted directly through the earth or water as a pressure wave and understood, either directly from the medium, or after simple amplification. The simplified waveform can be easily encoded by scrambling to provide secure voice communications. The simplified waveform may be used to operate machinery, produces more efficient public address systems and transmitters with greater range peak power for a given average power, and thus longer ranges.

In accordance with the present invention, the speech waveform is converted to a signal having substantially constant upper and lower levels with abrupt transitions from one level to the other, the abrupt transitions being in time correspondence to amplitude changes in the speech waveform that exceed a predetermined rate of change. This is accomplished by a system including a high-pass filter and means for converting the filtered waveform to a constant amplitude, substantially square wave.

More specifically, optimum results have been achieved by using a filter having a 12 decibel per octave slope from 0 to 15,000 cycles per second. In one specific embodiment, this filter is formed by a pair of tuned amplifier circuits each having a 6 decibel per octave slope within the frequency range of interest. In this embodiment, the speech waveform is preferably combined with a high frequency noise masking signal of lower amplitude prior to processing.

In accordance with another specific aspect of the invention, means for converting the filtered signal to a square wave comprises at least one amplifier followed by a clipper circuit.

The invention also contemplates a voice communication system having a plurality of separate channels within a bandwidth normally allotted for a single frequency, for example four channels within a bandwidth of 1,500 cycles per second. In this system the processed speech is selectively passed through one of a plurality of narrow band-pass filters to a

from a microphone (not illustrated) or other suitable transducer. The speech waveform is summed with a much higher frequency, for example 50 kHz, masking signal produced by the signal generator 14. This signal is passed through a pair of tuned amplifier circuits 16 and 18. Each of the circuits 16 and 18 is a high-pass filter having a 6 decibel per octave slope from 0 to 15,000 cycles per second, thus providing a combined slope of 12 decibels per octave.

The filtered waveform is then passed through a circuit means for converting the filtered waveform to a square wave which is comprised of a first high gain amplifier 20, a first clipper circuit 22, a second high gain amplifier 24, and a second clipper circuit 26. The square wave is then passed through power amplifier 28 to the output in a form to drive a loudspeaker, transducer, radio transmitter or the like. When ultimately passed through a speaker, or other suitable transducer, the square wave is fully intelligible. The square wave so produced has constant upper and lower levels, with very abrupt transitions between the upper and lower levels as a result of the two stages of amplification and clipping. The transitions occur in time correspondence to amplitude changes in the original speech waveform applied to the input 12 that exceed a predetermined rate of change so as to be passed through the high-pass filters 16 and 18.

A detailed circuit diagram of the system 10 is shown in FIG. 2 wherein corresponding components are designated by corresponding reference numerals. Each of the components is of conventional design. The signal generator 14 has a variable load resistor 30 in the output stage which permits the amplitude of the masking signal to be adjusted to eliminate oscillations caused by noise. The amplitude of the masking signal should not be any greater than is required to prevent oscillation to minimize interference with the processing of the speech waveform. The tuned amplifier circuits 16 and 18 are of identical construction. Each is comprised of an amplifier having a differential input stage 32 and a single output stage 34 which drives a tuned filter circuit 36. The tuned amplifier circuits 16 and 18 are coupled by capacitor 38, which of

3,647,970

3

course also comprises an element of the filter. The amplifier 20 is identical to the amplifier portions of the tuned amplifiers 16 and 18, and is coupled to the output of tuned amplifier 18 by capacitor 40. The clipper circuit 22 is merely a diode bridge coupled to the output of amplifier 20 by capacitor 42, followed by a filter comprised of capacitor 44 and resistor 46. The output of the clipper circuit 22 is coupled to the input of amplifier 24 by capacitor 48. Clipper 26 is identical to clipper 22 and is coupled to the output of amplifier 24 by capacitor 50. Amplifier 28 is identical to amplifiers 20 and 24 and is coupled to the output of the clipper circuit 26 by capacitor 52.

In a typical embodiment of the circuit of FIG. 2, the PNP-transistors may be MPS3640 transistors, the NPN-transistors may be MPS3393 transistors, and the diodes may be IN914 diodes. The resistors have the following values in kilohms as referenced in circuits 16 and 22: $a=33$, $b=33$, $c=10$, $d=33$, $e=0.33$, $f=33$, $g=10$, $h=10$, $i=10$, $j=100$, $k=100$, and $m=1.0$. The capacitors are 10 microfarads, except for the capacitors in the LC tuned circuits which are 0.001 microfarads. All coils are 10 millihenrys.

The high-pass filters 16 and 18 may be of any suitable conventional circuit design, and may be a resistor-capacitor filter, a shorted delay line filter, or an inductor-capacitor filter, for example. The means for converting the filtered waveform to a square wave may also be any suitable conventional circuit such as a Schmidt trigger, or a very high gain amplifier which quickly saturates.

A multichannel speech transmission system in accordance with the present invention is indicated generally by the reference numeral 60 in the schematic block diagram of FIG. 3. In the system 60, the speech processor 10 is selectively connectable to any one of four filters 62–65 by a selector switch 66. The outputs of the filters 62–65 are connected to the input of a conventional single side band transmitter 68.

4

mined by the polarity of the transition and are therefore passed through a fullwave rectifier 104 which converts all of the spike pulses to the same polarity. The spike pulses are then used to trigger a single shot multivibrator 106 which produces a pulse of predetermined amplitude and time width in response to each spike pulse. The uniform pulses from the single shot multivibrator 106 are then passed through an encoder 108 which produces a plurality of pulses of corresponding width in a predetermined timed sequence in response to each input pulse. This may easily be accomplished by a plurality of parallel delay lines d_0, d_1, and d_2 for transferring the pulses to point 110 at predetermined time intervals. The pulses are then amplified by an amplifier 112 which drives a transducer 114. The transducer 114 may induce the pulses in water, in the earth, or in any other propagating medium. Or if desired, the transducer 114 can be replaced by a radio or other electromagnetic wave transmitter.

The transmitted pulses are received by an appropriate receiving transducer 116, which reproduces electrical pulses of corresponding width and amplitude. The received pulses are amplified by amplifier 118 and applied to a decoder 120. The decoder 120 is comprised of an identical number of delay lines of identical time relationship so that the three pulses are recombined as a single pulse at summation point 122. Each time that the three pulses occur at the same point in time, the sum of the pulses exceeds the threshold of a detector 124 which triggers a flip-flop 126. The output of the flip-flop is then a reproduction of the square wave originally produced by the speech processor 10. This square wave is then amplified by amplifier 128 to drive a speaker 130 and produce the voice communication. Reproduction of the voice communication can be accomplished only if the receiving decoder matches the transmitting encoder. The encoders and decoders can be easily changed as required in order to maintain secure transmissions.

ble conventional design having mutually exclusive pass bands of about 300 cycles centered at frequencies f_1, f_2, f_3 and f_4, and are grouped within a total bandwidth of about 1,500 cycles, for example. Since 3,000 cycles is a typical bandwidth for single side band transmitters operated for simple speech transmission, eight filters can be used if desired. The square wave produced by the speech processor 10 may be selectively passed through any one of the narrow band-pass filters 62-65 without materially reducing its intelligibility.

The filtered square wave is transmitted by the conventional transmitter 68 to a conventional single side band receiver 70. The output of the receiver 70 is selectively connectable through filters 72-75 by a selector amplifier 78 by a selector switch 76. The filters 72-75 have corresponding passbands centered at frequencies f_1, f_2, f_3 and f_4. The amplifier 78 may drive a speaker 80. Therefore, if the selector switch 76 of a particular receiving set 70 is set to the filter corresponding in frequency to the filter selected by switch 66 in the transmitter, the filtered square wave will be reproduced by the speaker 80 and will be sufficiently intelligible for nearly all voice communication purposes. However, if the selector switch 76 of a particular receiver is set to another frequency filter, no sound is produced by the speaker 80. Thus, the transmission system of FIG. 3 provides four separate voice channels within the frequency band of 1,500 cycles, or eight channels in the 3,000 cycle bandwidth conventionally allotted for single side band operation. Of course, it is to be understood that the particular radio frequency is merely illustrative of the broader concept of the invention and that the same principles can be applied to transmissions through any media by electrical or electromagnetic waves.

A secure system for transmitting scrambled voice communications is indicated generally by the reference numeral 100 in FIG. 4. Again the speech processor 10 is used to generate the square wave as heretofore described. The square wave is then passed through a differentiator 102 which produces a sharp spike pulse in time correspondence to each transition of the square wave. The sharp spike pulses have a polarity deter-

Although preferred embodiments of the invention have been described in detail, it is to be understood that various changes, substitutions and alterations can be made therein without departing from the spirit and scope of the invention as defined by the appended claims.

What is claimed is:

1. The method for simplifying a speech waveform which comprises producing a signal having constant upper and lower levels with abrupt transitions from one level to the other, the abrupt transitions being in time correspondence to amplitude changes in the speech waveform that exceed a predetermined rate of change.

2. The method for simplifying a speech waveform which comprises:

passing the waveform through a high-pass filter, then converting the filtered waveform to a square wave of constant amplitude.

3. The method defined in claim 2 wherein the high-pass filter has a slope of about twelve decibels per octave in the frequency range of interest.

4. The method for transmitting speech which comprises:

producing an electrical waveform representative of the pressure waves produced by speech,

passing the electrical waveform through a high-pass filter to produce a first filtered signal,

converting the filtered waveform to a square waveform of constant amplitude, and

driving a speaker with the square waveform.

5. The method defined in claim 4 wherein:

the square waveform is transmitted as a pressure wave prior to being used to drive a speaker.

6. The method defined in claim 4 wherein:

the square waveform is transmitted by electromagnetic wave propagation prior to being used to drive a speaker.

7. The method defined in claim 4 wherein:

the square waveform is converted to a series of time related pulses, and the time related pulses are transmitted to another locale and converted back to a square waveform which is used to drive the speaker.

3,647,970

5

8. The method defined in claim 4 wherein the square waveform is passed through a band-pass filter having a center frequency in the audio range prior to being used to drive the speaker.

9. The system for simplifying a speech waveform which comprises:

means for for producing a speech waveform,

high-pass filter means for filtering the speech waveform, and

means for converting the filtered waveform to a constant amplitude square wave.

10. The system defined in claim 9 wherein the filter means has a slope of about twelve decibels per octave in the frequency range of interest.

11. The system defined in claim 10 wherein the filter means is two filter circuits in series each having a slope of about 6 decibels per octave.

12. The system defined in claim 11 wherein each filter means includes an amplifier followed by a tuned circuit.

13. The system defined in claim 9 wherein the means for converting the filtered waveform to a constant amplitude square wave is at least one stage comprised of an amplifier and means for limiting the amplitude of the output of the amplifier.

14. The system defined in claim 13 wherein the means for converting the filtered waveform to a constant amplitude square wave is two stages connected in series, each stage comprising an amplifier and means for limiting the amplitude of the output of the amplifier.

6

15. The system defined in claim 9 further characterized by: at least two band-pass filter means having different pass bands in the audio range for filtering the square wave, transmitter means for transmitting an audio range signal, and

switch means for passing the square wave through a selected band-pass filter means to the transmitter means.

16. The system defined in claim 9 further characterized by: means for converting the square wave to a series of pulses occurring in a predetermined time relationship to at least a portion of the transitions of the square wave, and

means for transmitting the pulses.

17. The system defined in claim 16 wherein the means for converting the square wave to a series of pulses comprises:

means for producing a first set of pulses of predetermined amplitude and time duration, each pulse corresponding in time to a transition of the square wave, and

encoder means for producing a plurality of pulses in predetermined time relationship for each pulse of the first set of pulses.

18. The system defined in claim 17 wherein the encoder means comprises:

at least two parallel paths for the pulses of the first set having different propagation periods.

19. The system defined in claim 16 further characterized by: means for receiving the pulses and converting the pulses back to a square wave having time correspondence to the original square wave.

* * * * *